Steeped

A Big Sur Elixir of Sulfur and Sage

by
Brita Ostrom
Esalen® Legacy Practitioner

Steeped: A Big Sur Elixir of Sulfur and Sage

© Copyright 2025 Brita Ostrom

ISBN: 978-0989523455
Library of Congress Control Number: 2025946437

All rights reserved. No part of this book may be reproduced in any form or by any electronic or mechanical means, including information storage and retrieval systems, without written permission from the author, except in the case of a reviewer, who may quote brief passages embodied in critical articles or in a review.

Trademarked names may appear throughout this book. Rather than use a trademark symbol with every occurrence of a trademarked name, names are used in an editorial fashion, with no intention of infringement of the respective owner's trademark.

Cover Photo Credit: Horst Mayer
Back Cover Sketch: Paul O'Rourke
Big Sur Musical Gathering Painting: Marian Scott
Doorway Photo: Daniel Bost
Isabel Allende quote used by permission
Esalen® is a registered mark of the Esalen Institute, Big Sur, CA 93920

Published by

845 Main Street, Morro Bay, CA 93442
Submissions to Coalesce Press by invitation only.

v25-0905

*In a memoir you are trying to reach some kind of truth,
something that is true to you.*

~ Isabel Allende

*Dedicated to those who walk this earth
while gazing at the stars.*

TABLE OF CONTENTS

PRELUDE: SUMMER OF LOVE...7
INTRODUCTION: ESALEN'S DRUMBEAT SIRENS................................15
DREAMTIME STARTED WITH RIP VAN WINKLE..............................19
NO SLEEP TONIGHT: HOT SPRINGS CANYON 1967.......................25
THE NUMBER ONE ROUTE HOME 33
MY FIRST BATH...37
DID DICK PRICE RUN BY HERE? 39
NO MORE NICE GIRL 49
COMPETITION AND CONNECTION 55
LOOK, IT'S GEORGE LEONARD...61
ESALEN® MASSAGE: ADDING LAYERS 63
I WORE FLOWERS IN MY HAIR WHEN I MET THE ANTI-HIPPIE LARS..67
FULL MOON IN AUGUST 75
THE LION SPEAKS TONIGHT: CHANGING NAMES..........................79
DROPPING OUT 87
EAVESDROPPING 95
EXILED AGAIN IN BIG SUR...97
WE HIKE CASTRO RANCH AND DON'T GET SHOT......................105
A LOCAL VOLCANO: GRANDPA DEETJEN 107
A RESCUE FROM TOO HIGH 113
AT HOME IN A TREE 117
WHERE GIANTS PLAY 123
THE EDGY CANYON OF NATURAL LOVE 129
I WAS THE SECRET IN MY FAMILY 137
UNTIE THIS VOW 141

STEAL THIS CHEESE: END THE WAR	143
TENT RAISING	149
WINTER IN BIG SUR	155
LEAVING TO ARRIVE: THE LONG WALK	161
UNMAPPED DEPARTURE	165
A BEND IN ROUTE ONE	173
FEELING OUT LOUD	177
SEX WILL SAVE US	183
TOUCH ME HEAL ME	187
GIVING A MASSAGE	193
AFFIRMATION FROM THE ASTRAL PLANE	197
HOW DO YOU END A CHAPTER	199
ABOUT THE AUTHOR	203
ABOUT COALESCE PRESS	205

Prelude: Summer of Love

"San Francisco here we come!" my mustached husband Bob belted out our theme song as we crossed the Bay Bridge. Not a minute later he yanked on the brake and slid the key out of the ignition of our getaway vehicle, a white van on delivery to the Stella Dora Cookie Factory, Halloween, 1966. He faced me and grinned, "We're here." I giggled with relief and he joined in, his laughter booming. A few costumed children sitting on a nearby curb looked up, then got back to their serious work of counting out their candy loot.

We slowly unfurled our tired bodies out of the cab and plopped down near them. San Francisco. I inhaled the moist air and caught a hint of eucalyptus scent from an oversized tree on the corner, bark dangling unkempt from its naked limbs. Who knew air could smell this good? The biting fragrance cleared my nasal passages. I stretched my legs out and scanned the *San Francisco Chronicle* want ads looking for our new home.

"Let's check this one out," Bob nuzzled my ear as he pointed at a "for rent" notice on Shrader Street, with a Private Entrance. We hopped back in the truck and pointed it westward. The landlord wanted one hundred dollars a month, and we were in no position to bargain. Done deal! At daybreak we unloaded our few belongings and our very scared young cat into our new garden apartment with its own hinged white gate three blocks off Haight Street, our target destination. When we dropped the truck off at the cookie factory just before the deadline, I took a grateful backward glance at this shiny van that had ferried us three-thousand miles from New York City to this proclaimed land of free everything: The Haight Street District. We inhaled the roses blooming outside our bedroom window on this November morning. Good-bye East Coast winter gloom.

Prelude: Summer of Love

"C'mon Sweetie." Bob's eyes focused ahead, and he outpaced me once he spotted the Blue Unicorn Coffee House sign a block away down Hayes Street. We swung open a heavy door into its cavernous interior, dark, but not as dingy as our familiar hang-out on New York's Lower East Side. The walls were lined with faded magazine covers. The dusty storefront bay windows provided space for local rags like last week's issue of the *Berkeley Barb* and a collection of dog-eared paperbacks. A half-eaten Snickers bar still in the wrapper peeked from beneath a faded hardback copy of *One Flew Over the Cuckoo's Nest*.

"Hey." The tired young man behind the counter greeted us flatly without looking up. We ordered two coffees, one with cream, one without. He took his time drawing it from the large drip pot. "Sit anywhere." He gave us change from the dollar Bob pulled from his pants' pocket and waved us away. The few customers, mostly young men, sat hunkered down over faded books or engaged in playfully combative conversation. They looked like they lived there. A black and white chess set sat ready on its own table.

"Anybody here play chess?" Bob raised his voice above the din and scanned the room as he headed to the table and plunked down his coffee. He immediately hustled up a game with the one short-haired kid in the place. "Pawn to king four," Bob clicked the pawns onto the wooden board. The kid looked baffled by this noisy bravado, and blew his third move, creating an easy pathway to checkmate. Bob didn't hesitate to express his disappointment at his partner's lack of skill. "Where'd you learn how to play?" he asked derisively, then laughed. "Oh well, we'll try it again later." He pushed his chair out and stood up. He had a South Jersey accent, and it shown forth here in his aggressive repartee. We were definitely new to the neighborhood. Those at the table behind us drew their chairs back and looked away.

We ordered the daily special, beef stew, while we listened to a stringy-haired young man tune his guitar and sing inaudible home-grown lyrics. I frowned. "No rules here," smiled a young woman dining nearby. "Anybody can sing." Our eager inquiry about a rumored concert tour was met with, "Bob Dylan? He sold out to electric music."

We created our home in our Haight Ashbury apartment: single mattress on the bedroom floor with windows open to the garden, slightly used TV-turntable combo in the living room fronting the low-slung orange couch and enameled black coffee table carted out from New York. Our kitty curled up, cozy. Word got out about our cool pad. In no time at all, our first guests arrived, Bill and Drena, young pals from New York. Bob spread his arms wide in welcome and joked, "Look what the cat just dragged in from Brooklyn!" and I made coffee and peanut butter sandwiches with grape jelly. They stayed two months.

We opened our living room doors to more friends and even to strangers who heeded the call to San Francisco's *Flower Power*. One of them left old Indian baskets from the Pueblo; another stole our portable radio and mailed us the pawn ticket. At The Unicorn, we shared our table with a stubble-faced young guy from Colorado with wandering eyes and a rumpled man just in from Seattle. The place filled up and Herb the owner ran out of soup.

Truth was, all this love in the coffee houses and on the streets made us a little uncomfortable. So much smiling, who could you trust? Even the police smiled here. We were accustomed to East Coast tougher love, a surly snarl and lifted chin to defy authority. Here in windy San Francisco, any sign of a raised voice or clenched jaw was promptly deemed aggressive by local peace and love advocates. They berated us for our well-honed street survival skills. "What now? Love the Pigs?" Bob dismissed. We arrived well-defended: it would take months for my body to unwind after New York's Lower East Side tough-girl posture, to drop my shoulders and dance freely to music in the San Francisco's Panhandle Park.

Bob maintained his chesty stance and his high laced workman's boots. He openly gawked at the girls and was shocked one night to fondle a guy's balls underneath the short skirt. Breasts gleamed, liberated from cotton brassieres. Loose Mexican pants let it all hang out. Sex seemed everywhere available but with a new set of rituals and no guidebook. A local rag, The *San*

Prelude: Summer of Love

Francisco Oracle's centerfold girl sat naked, proudly pregnant, the promise of a natural life. Privately, I was bewildered by the combo of our married status in this land of winks and breasts and an uninvited caress in the line for coffee.

Yes, love was in the air, re-painting a gray working-class neighborhood with rainbow prisms. A magical mist hung over our new wake up spot, the I and Thou coffeehouse, just a block from the street corner of Haight and Ashbury. Bob played chess while I read *the Chronicle* or strolled in nearby Golden Gate Park. We lunched late on the Blue Unicorn's soup special, with its permanent row of broken-down VW vans parked outside. Look! People from all over were coming, affirming our vision. *Make love, not war. Get out of Vietnam. A psychedelic revolution!* In no time, artisan shops sprung up, nudging out a Polish Deli where I had ordered piroshki. Freshly painted storefront signs designated Haight Street commerce: The brassy Psychedelic Shop sat next to a tiny storefront health food store selling dark and sticky unrefined sugar. The Psychedelic Shop window was devoted to the ways and means of getting high, with hookahs and rolling papers and crystals. Bob and I frowned; our secret culture of smoking pot on the fire escape was out in the open and for sale here. Was this legal? I scratched my head and glanced at the store's customers. I was surprised to see books for sale. *Island* by Huxley sat centered on the front shelf.

Bob and I settled in. I gave up the notion of finding meaningful social work in a crazy world. We no longer attended the violent peace rallies in Berkeley. Now we hunkered down and tried to learn this new vocabulary of love and immediacy. "Make Haight Street your yoga," advised Richard Alpert aka Ram Das. What did this require of me? What kindness, what charity, what imagination? While a spontaneous rally in Golden Gate Park might include an accented communist on his soap box, for the most part we danced; we cheered musicians on their way to the big time; we looped chalk drawings on the sidewalk. We met our neighbors. I began to relax my stance. Bob liked this new me, but he eyed every new setting suspiciously before breaking into a smile and joining in.

I versed myself in the day's horrific current events: the war machine, the killing, and the sacrifices my friends were making to de-escalate the conflict in Vietnam. But fighting the war with more fighting just didn't make sense. The only thing we could trust was each other, this new set of crewmates we now sailed with. We went home only to sleep. We wanted to taste what was new, who arrived today, hear the new song. Bob and I became less intimate together; Late night, I spilled out my feelings, hopes and doubts to the newest seeker at the remodeled Drugstore Café.

We also trusted puff the magic dragon, "Feed your head." When I took mescaline or LSD on the East Coast, I never did it socially. I always carefully curated the setting. Out west, dilated eyes and lucid laughter rang forth on the street, in eatery antics, in wildly gesturing conversation. I envied the uninhibited girl under the tree who danced slowly to her own music. I tossed my shoes to get my toes into the earth. I felt the glow of spirit all around me and learned to bask in the presence of eye-to-eye contact. I wanted to know who was inside. This was a new kind of personal power, and we were encouraged to act it out. A colony of Hopis, Sufis, LA cowboys, gurus, and beautiful babes spring up around us.

These shared acid trips, artisan business ventures, and deep conversation over espresso or in bed led to our bonded community. Hippies. When I walked down the street I knew who to trust to ask for help and I knew if the Diggers were feeding the homeless or if we needed to look out for that runaway boy who arrived yesterday. We took care of ourselves; we challenged ourselves to laugh at our inhibitions.

The tribes gathered that winter for the first Human Be-in. "Fear will be washed away, ignorance will be exposed to sunlight, profits and empire will lie drying on deserted beaches, violence with be submerged and transmuted in rhythm and dancing...." Proclaimed the *Berkeley Barb*, January 15, 1967. Of course, we went. Of course, our minds were blown by the sheer numbers. Twenty thousand people showed up and heard the siren opening blasts of Gary Snyder's white-beaded conch shell call us into being. We weren't alone anymore.

Prelude: Summer of Love

I jotted down my thoughts in a January, 1967, letter to my college friend Miki. "Did I tell you about the Be-in? A giant gathering in Golden Gate Park of the Psychedelics and the Politicos--beautiful people everywhere from everywhere. Ginsburg, Leary, Alpert, Berkeley radicals and some great electric guitar music." I recalled how we sat very close to the Hells Angels, grateful for their protective stance. Wait a minute. Now we needed protection, in a town where "love" was the password? Yet this move from our outsider defensive stance to today's inside participation flipped my head. Yesterday's rebellion had overnight become today's lifestyle—in Haight Ashbury, a land unto itself.

In spring of the so-called summer of love I turned twenty-three, tossed my untrimmed long blond hair, and stepped into a sleek sparkly short dress I designed and sewed for myself. I was ready to go dancing at Winterland, or at the Avalon Ballroom, or at the Straight Theater. I put a clear light window pane of LSD under my tongue and I threw myself into the music and the vivid lightshow throbbing photos across the walls and the dance floor. I rediscovered my vestigial dinosaur wings, I spun and loved the dizziness. A dancer on the stage was our muse as she swung her fringed bolero and high-stepping boots. I fell into kinship with dancers everywhere: in Asia, in Bali, anywhere that dance led to an ecstatic connection with spirit. We bumped into each other, we fell in love on the dance floor, we parted company and cried when the music ended. Big brother and the Holding Company brought us the psychedelic slow melodic beat, Janis Joplin screamed, and a dozen youthful bands brought us to our knees. All music demanded movement, dance, emotion. No one ever squatted down and just sat passively on their madras spread. That would be capitalistic, ownership. The Haight demanded full participation to join its community. One afternoon in the Panhandle I blocked a photographer who thought he could just look. I led the clean-shaven man with his lens cap off this way and that until he was forced to join the fun.

The summer of love turned out to be foggy. It was not an insider's summer of love. The bands were better, the crowds were bigger. Every high school senior in San Francisco made a secret trip to this new world in their midst. We saw them, wild eyed and stoned. I yearned to help guide them but there were just too many. I was lost in the crowd. So were they. The Haight Ashbury clinic swung into full time operation with a room-sized message board about runaways and missing people and VD. The Diggers packed up their storefront outreach, declared Haight Ashbury dead, and advised us to move out to the country.

In the process, Bob moved one direction and I moved another. I wrote my friend Miki, "The San Francisco Haight Street scene is dead, gone to the hustlers and the youngsters who, although beautiful, come in numbers so large that they became confused by their own numbers and by the myth." I furrowed my brows.

Sunday afternoon I relaxed at home, listening to the local public radio station. Alan Watts was speaking, and I leaned in closer. I'd owned his book, *Psychotherapy East and West*, since high school and sought his seminal insights on psychology and religion. His crisp British accent filled the airwaves. He ended today's talk with a headline, "I'm at the Esalen Institute this week." I immediately put a thumb tack in my imaginary map. This was a place I needed to check out. Big Sur. An old beatnik place. Alan Watts. The Esalen Institute. My curiosity spun into overdrive.

We took the neighborhood advice. Keep moving. We gave up our spacious garden apartment. We sprouted new relationships while not quite saying good-bye. My husband crossed the country with a leggy blonde in the front seat. I walked hand in hand with my new pal, Paul, through Golden Gate Park. Smitten, he and I experimented with hitch-hiking, first tackling the Golden Gate Bridge to Marin. You might see me in an old black and white photo: smiling directly at the camera, slender, wearing sandals and restyled jeans; he's got a beard, dingy white pants and a bright sweater. We lean forward, thumbs held high; we are empty handed, hitching down Bridgeway Street in Sausalito, bound for a pal on the houseboats or an adventure we haven't imagined yet. Next day, we pointed our thumbs south, to Big Sur. To Esalen.

Prelude: Summer of Love

We took our dreams of love and peace and art with us. I carried a small duffle with a blanket.

Introduction: Esalen's Drumbeat Sirens

As an adult remembers childhood landscapes from a pint-size reference point rendering the world large, so my initial visit to Esalen appeared as a massive spread of lawn, bleached redwood buildings, very colorful people, and the downhill gash of Hot Springs Creek rushing to join the ocean. The geo-mass of the Santa Lucia Mountains sliding into the Pacific slowed here on this remote ledge inhabited a millennium ago by the Esselen tribe. Today's site stood re-imaged as a steamy hot springs hotel sponsoring seminars on *The Further Reaches of Human Potentiality*.

I clamored my way out of the back seat of the Dented VW van that responded to our outstretched thumbs with a lift to Big Sur. At last we spotted the road sign: Big Sur Hot Springs. Paul tossed our bed rolls onto the dusty driveway, I just. Stopped. Moving. I sank my travel-weary body gratefully into the thick lawn and found it springy. Time fell away. The blueness of the sea and sky rested my eyes, the spongy grass tickled my toes, and the paisley-clad locals welcomed us into an alternative reality. With an exhausted sigh, I dropped to the earth, and I rolled on that grassy carpet all the way down to the cliff's edge. The seascape reflected the curvature of our planet and a cloud-free technicolor blue sky arched overhead. I rolled past a drummer beating out a Latin rhythm on his conga. A blonde woman in a swinging blue skirt danced lightly nearby. I rolled past two paunchy gents with towels flung over their shoulders. A laughing couple strode by, his white Mexicali shirt setting off his chest, her long dark hair flying with their movement. She wore her pregnancy proudly. Accustomed to voluminous smocks cloaking the obvious belly I marveled at this comfort with female fecundity.

Introduction: Esalen's Drumbeat Sirens

A ten-year-old girl with cascading yellow curls pointed at me and sharply warned, "Look out for the big rock!" just in time for me to open my eyes and dodge a flaky chunk of granite. I rolled to a stop and rubbed the lawn off my face.

Asia lay somewhere in the mist in front of me and the upcropping striated stone of the Santa Lucia range backed me. Fatigue from this summer's Haight street home and the stress of a recent trip through the Chicano Grape strike *Huelga!* had frayed my nerves. Now I gratefully closed my eyes, and the ocean song did its work. I didn't notice the lone ant that took his time exploring my left foot. Maybe it's true, maybe this coastal air holds extra oxygen. When I sensed the late afternoon coolness, I blinked my eyes open to an orange-streaked sunset world more appropriate to the big screen than daily life.

My unkempt hair hung tangled around my shoulders and leaves fell from my cut-off jeans as I stood up on this tickly grass. Old handmade sandals didn't protect my feet. Paul wore his singular belongings after months of living on the road: his raggedy red wool ski sweater that somehow still looked neat around the collar and cuffs; loose white pants now graying, and oversized sneakers. I'd trimmed his straw-colored beard and his softly curling hair just last week, and it was already shaggy. His body leaned into motion, legs slightly askew from years of horseback riding. Now he playfully shouted "Gotcha!" leaping in the air, aiming his cocked finger at me, and then crashing dramatically into the grass when I returned fire. He'd been a stunt man in Westerns and he knew a dozen ways to die. I dove and fell, laughing, abandoning myself to this man, this grass, this place. A young kid joined us, eager to meet these latest newcomers. Spying our gear, he pointed out a nearby eucalyptus tree and advised, "You can sleep there tonight. Just lay low."

I brushed myself off. Paul jumped up and we let gravity direct our steps downward, ending up on a cliffside point anchored by unruly cypress trees jutting over the ocean. Sitting beneath the closer tree on a log was a lone woman, solemnly smoking. "Hey," she beckoned us. "Come over here, have a toke" and waved her rolled joint in the air. "My medicine," she said, looking at it.

"Spirit sends us all this." She looked right at us now. Her straight gray hair fell down her stout body and framed her round face. She was plain dressed in a faded loose cotton jumper that covered her legs. She pointed to herself, "Lorna," and said she washed vegetables in the kitchen. "Lot of brothers and sisters already here, pay attention." Her eyes twinkled and she almost smiled before she regained her reverent mood. I learned later that she was barely forty. In this moment, she seemed as old as these hills.

Awed by her humbleness, I found no words for conversation. Her quiet speech rang with an authority that comes from living life based on her own principles. "Sacrament," she pronounced, striking a wooden match on a nearby rock to reignite the marijuana. I was nervous about smoking openly but didn't want to miss out. She advised us to "Respect this smoke and those who came to this land before." Indeed, as we passed the joint, those Native Peoples seemed very close, perhaps living in cliffside caves or in the hollowed out Redwood trees just up the canyon.

I perched on a stump; Paul squatted on the ground; Lorna balanced comfortably on her log. We sat in symphonic silence, as salty waves defined the edge of the continental cliffs below us. To our north, Hot Springs Creek waterfall spilled bridal showers over rocks in the deep canyon on its race to the Pacific. A light breeze swung the cypress boughs overhead. The moist air hung thick and fragrant around us. "Had twin sons," she broke the silence. "Lost both of 'em in 'Nam a few months apart. Spirit sent me here." My stomach dropped at her words. Paul nodded and rocked his body back. I rolled my eyes downward, respecting her loss and admiring her strength to just speak it. When I looked up at her, she met my eyes for a second, rose and walked slowly and silently away. Her long dress caught the wind.

"Heavy," said Paul.

"Yeah," I sighed.

Twilight faded. We rose and moved into the candle-lit Esalen dining lodge. Paul poured himself a coffee while I focused on a small troupe of musicians including some of the same drummers. The pregnant woman now danced a sinuous solo. As the drums beat faster two other women leapt up, shadows flying off their twisting skirts. The beat changed into a seductive syncopation reminiscent of Cuba. Those guests at the nearby tables at first watched quizzically, tapping their feet, then slowly joined in, their limbs clearly unaccustomed to such broad movement, grimacing, grinning, trying this dance floor for the first time. Some kept their eyes closed tight to better feel the beat.

I wasn't sure if this resembled a pre-history past or a future dream community. As it turned out, tonight's mythic gathering was part of an advanced training group with the noted Gestalt Psychiatrist, Fritz Perls. The assignment was to get into the music, the movement, to dance the dance of creation. I too joined in, inviting the drums to find rhythms through my torso I had never experienced before. When the fireplace showed only glowing embers, I flung my head back and laughed. *Do it now, become alive, say it with your body.*

Under the brightest stars I'd ever seen, we followed the kid's advice, stretching out our sleeping rolls beneath the tree and settled into our own communicating with spirit, punctuated by deep intakes of breath and satisfied sighs. This place, this man with nothing but his antics and his lightheartedness, this is what I had dropped into. The Milky Way spanned the entire breadth of the sky with more stars than I'd ever witnessed before.

As the summer of love rolled to a foggy close in San Francisco, I found it easy to pack a few clothes and tell my husband I was on a quest. I quit my UC Med Center secretary job and skipped the next anti-war demonstration to join this effervescent community that challenged me with their hugs, their fearless personal exploration, and their ability to live on the steep hills. No wonder Fritz said he came because of the place, "The mountain and the sea coming together and lovely community, such beautiful people." I could not have stayed home.

Dreamtime Started with Rip Van Winkle

Rip Van Winkle has nothing on me. I stayed in this steamy Big Sur dream for fifty years. In fact, a lot of preliminary tuning up to get here had begun in Rip Van Winkle's actual back yard, the Catskill Mountains. In summer,1965, Bob and I became better acquainted by dropping LSD near Sleepy Hollow while camping with friends. This was blotter acid, a small magic dose of homemade lysergic acid dripped onto colored paper. The dosage was wildly uneven, though we thought it measured about 350 micrograms. I placed the small torn square of paper on my tongue and waited. "Feel anything?" asked Bob, ever the skeptic. The night brightened and began to bend. I giggled and basked in the greenness around me.

"I'm so thirsty!" I soon exclaimed. Bob sniffed around, took a few wobbly steps, sniffed again. Like in a dream, he felt around and found a working water facet, and with delight we cupped the liquid in our hands, splashed our faces. We drank that sweet water and I knew. Anyone who could discover water had to be the one for me.

I drank the water all night long. My debut journey into an alternate reality started by experiencing disintegration all around me. The trees dissolved and bent this way and that; the leaves showed me their cellular structure; the ground rose up and met my feet. At times I became so heavy I could barely stand. I identified with stones and peered at them, felt my connection to the mineral crystals and the earth. I rose and moved with the wind, letting it lift me. Bob and I laughed like children. "We'll still play like this when we're sixty, "we vowed laughingly. As the trip ended, the trees resumed their tree-like structure; yet they remained close to me, protecting me, visibly pulsating with life.

Next morning, we travelled in our friends' old Chevy sedan to nearby Castalia Foundation in Millbrook, New York. This would become ground zero of the psychedelic experience, modeled on ousted Harvard Professors Richard Albert and Timothy Leary's seminal book by the same name. We rolled up to a Dutch colonial house bordered by an even older building set further back. In our wide-eyed psychedelic spaciousness, we tromped around and found no one. "Look at this, Brita!" called Bob, and swung open the Dutch door of the older building.

Ascending the creaky stairs, we stumbled into a cobweb-strung bowling alley, wooden balls and antique ten-pins intact. Sunlight slanted through leaded glass panes illuminating the floating dust particles. I impulsively grabbed a ball, swung my arm back, then sprang it forward to roll toward the pins. The loud rumble shook more dust loose. I watched as the ball descended down its lane and knocked three of the ten pins over. Washington Irving's adage, *thunder is the sound of the Gods bowling* must be true. We had entered a God realm.

We crossed the driveway to the main house, passing a hammock occupied by a slender young woman in full recline, her dark hair and India-print skirt draping down. "What a beautiful woman!" breathed Bob.

A quiet-spoken Ralph Metzner introduced himself at the entry, "Leary's pharmacologist. Please come in." I found a chair and joined the small assembly, discussing poppies in the fields outside Athens and the role of psychedelics in ancient Greek myth. Bob lingered by the door. Heady stuff! Had other cultures felt the necessity to get high, to go beyond everyday reality? Tim Leary held forth in another room, and we were not drawn to go in. I was disappointed that Richard Alpert was away that weekend. We were the youngsters in the crowd of older seekers, mainly psychologists and rich women who helped support the Institute.

Some of the attendees lived full-time at Castalia. One wrote in their journal, left out on a table, "We lived as a community of people who had accepted a certain way of living, which had rules and goals, shared by all. We felt that our life-style was a creative solution to the problems of living in the cinematic, labor-saving world. We wanted to explore our spiritual individuality, discover our secret life within, but also to test the validity of our search by means of living and loving and sharing with other people in close community."

I paused to look for Bob, but he had disappeared, in search of a bathroom. I read on. "It was some kind of heightened feeling of self …the texture and the music of natural surroundings, created a corresponding ambiance of colour, affective tonality, and seriousness in our minds. Here we could travel…to remote and hitherto inaccessible realms within. We sought the god who inhabits each and every man. We took this lofty house and turned it into a small stepping stone."

The journal's anonymous author spoke to my hope for shared dreams in a community of like-minded dwellers, of touching the inaccessible, of travel into our own minds. I had just met this man who could sniff out water. He and I grew closer and in less than three weeks decided to marry. Yet I longed for community, longed to tap my deeper resources and make art out of anti-war. After my disappointment with peace marches that called out, "End the War," and then chanted, referring to the approaching police, "Kill the pigs," I felt personally challenged to unmask the impulse that led us toward aggression and war. Happenings — unscripted dramatic events — were the rage back on campus and here I was, living one. We could drop into Rip Van Winkle's bowling alley, wander through unlocked doors, and be graciously welcomed just as we were while also challenged to dig deeper. This is the stuff my dreams were made of.

The following year, Bob and I left New York City and drove our few belongings west in that Stella D'Oro cookie truck driveaway. One of our cats ran away in Utah. We rode on toward the promise of Haight Ashbury and its *make love not war* mantra. Wide-eyed, we joined the hippies in their reverence for beauty, India block-print bedspreads, incense, and a belief in a spirit-imbued world. We rented our garden apartment and invited old friends and people we met on the street to sleep over. Even when one of them ripped off all our electronics, we just laughed and we danced in the park. A married couple still, I wanted to live in a unified community. Yet when we gave up the apartment, Bob and I lasted only one night in the communal *House of Peace and Love*. We quietly escorted ourselves out after the inhabitants judged us, "Too much stuff," because we had a couch, and the landlord implied he had sexual privileges with his female tenants.

A week later on Haight street a black man was stabbed on the sidewalk as Bob played chess in the Drugstore Café. "Go home," tersely whispered a passerby. "A load of horse (heroin) just came in and it's going to get rough."

I realized the magic of living free was over. The summer of love had been hijacked. Bob went his own way. As the nation hurled through the Vietnam war protests and the concurrent deals with aerospace companies, I had to speak up or better yet, act. I was bored with the Haight Street malaise: the world could end at any time so why do anything? I was eager to develop a new way to live, a more harmonious lifestyle. Behind the flower in my hair I had a mission. I was clueless how I would get there. Maybe this Esalen community would hold the answer.

The head shops lining the neighborhood sold individual glass beads, each type nestled in its small cubby, a hundred shapes and colors for us locals to string into beaded necklaces. I pondered over them, feeling their uneven roundness, holding them up the light to measure their translucence. I envisioned a strand representing my life with a bead for each phase: my childhood on an island community in salty Puget Sound searching for secret Indian treasure buried in the woods. This would be represented by seaglass. The fast dive into an Eastern Women's College with equal numbers of Black, Catholic, and Jewish students, with WASPS like me a minority. This would be represented by my favorite multicolored Venetian glass beads. I'd string the growing Civil rights movement pushing us to Washington DC to legislate change with tiny multi-stranded green African beads. Dull black clay beads interspersed with small red glass spacers represented our misguided war. My inner directive prompted me toward full throated expression and shared community art, adding an amethyst sparkle on my life strand. The next beads to string onto my necklace, right next to luminous pearl marriage bead, and just after the crystal prism of Haight Street, was Esalen, melting pot for East and West best represented by the large Peking-blue glass bead, widely traded up and down the west coast by Native peoples.

When I arrived on this springy lawn, LSD was still medicinally legal, a hope for those spiritually directed and a potent panacea for those whose minds howled with chaotic voices. As I looked left toward the high-rise mountains and right to the precipitous cliffs brooding over the sea, I felt my mind unhinge from thinking scared. My shoulders relaxed and my legs stilled. At Esalen, I didn't need to take anything to step into an altered reality. I rolled down the lawn one more time for good measure. Later that afternoon, I spied the woman in the hammock, last seen as Castalia. She lived here too.

No Sleep Tonight: Hot Springs Canyon 1967

I committed myself to walk this Big Sur land for a month as a rite of passage out of the city. Either the land would like me or it wouldn't. How would I know? Local lore told of Abe Maslow driving up Route One on a wintery night and hitting a small rock, resulting in a flattened tire just as he passed Esalen. Naturally he took this first opportunity to stop for help. He drove down the steep driveway and braked at the rustic gate shack. He'd never heard of this place. His interest was more than piqued when he spotted the gate guard reading the book he'd authored, *Toward a Psychology of Being*.

He ended up staying the night, forging a bond with staff who enthusiastically greeted him when he came to dine in the lodge. They plied him with questions about his concept of self-actualization, his map to developing one's full potential, a model of *go for it* living that hit home for them. His work broke with the pathology model of psychology — "you're sick, a psycho" — and instead looked at what fosters optimal development: honesty, awareness, freedom, trust, and that cherry on the top, peak experience.

That cherry caught Paul's attention. Although he carried very little, I'd spotted a dog-eared copy in his back pocket when we first met. He was no stranger to peak experiences, whether a creative blitz, a nuanced dramatic performance, or the peaks of the coast range. He threw himself with gusto into torturous long hikes with no map. I saw his eager strides; I'd seen emergent community potential on Haight Street, and in the peace movement. But for myself? Sure, this living outside the box was a step toward a different me. But to step all the way into my life, without hesitation or fear of standing out or slipping into sloth? That's a tough assignment even if the payoff was this cheery, self-actualization. Maybe this place would provide the magic.

Paul's voice called me to shake off worn-out social constraints. More than anyone I ever met he marched to his own drum. "On a clear day…Rise and look around you…" he sang out into the canyon and waited for his own echo. He penciled on a scrap of paper left in his paperback book: *"Whistling winds out there ~ Play a game of push and grab ~ Impossible to tame ~ Buffet winds push me to my knees ~ then watch me rise and skip along ~ in laughing cutting answer to your tease."*

Similarly, the Big Sur locals lived unabashedly poor, proud of what they created out of nothing in this land, proud of their art. When I joined them in dance, I too stood taller, full of myself, no posturing. They devoured self-discovery, even when it resulted in hurt, rejection or betrayal. The Esalen art barn was full of shattered pots and few museum-worthy glazed bowls that had withstood the critical potter's eye. The locals didn't need an audience to start the play; It emerged out of themselves. As I rose to partake in this unbridled joy, I muted myself, constrained by my need for safety, my fear of what others might think.

Tentatively, little by little I learned to meet each moment with my senses wide open. "Sniff out the possibilities," advised one teacher. I greeted my inner nay-sayers, and stepped beyond them. Scared? Sure! But soon I could taste this trail or try a new fruit or munch on a wild frond. The land won me over and invited me to stay.

The invitation included letting go of boundaries, otherwise known as trespassing. Here's a conversation from the future, five decades later.

We four women are dining at the Big Sur Inn in the fireplace room. French antiques and cracked china vases line the walls. We have known each other nearly 50 years. We have shared work, boyfriends, clothes, births, children, gossip, deaths, difficulties, and now we talk about the soul and about our heart problems. We are celebrating my birthday in style, and they will pick up my tab, just as I will pick up the tab for them later this year, 2018.

Steeped

"Did you really sleep under a bridge?" Peggy asks, sipping her glass of local chardonnay, catching me by surprise. My early history must have come up at an Esalen staff meeting, one that I failed to attend. She echoed my recent conversation with Michael Murphy, Esalen's co-founder.

He'd exclaimed, "Back then, hippies were sleeping under the bridge! Can you imagine?"

I'd replied, "Yes, I was one of them. I slept under the bridge." Word gets around.

What bridge?" she persisted. Hot Springs Creek Bridge. Part of Route One, the high bridge spanned a steep canyon. Back before this bridge was built by convicts in the 30's, the original Coast Road crossed on a smaller bridge far below, just a few feet above the creek that created this earthen gash. That old bridge still rested in place, but not firmly. This would be its last winter. The jubilant rush of clear water tumbled past its cement footings, swirled over granite boulders sculpted round by its steady force, created a frigid swimming hole, and then cascaded downward as the canyon floor dropped. A tepid spring wafted a slight sulfuric smell beside the stream bed. The creek abruptly dropped in a frothy 50-foot waterfall and dumped its spring-fresh water without further ado into the salty Pacific.

The "new" bridge spanned high above, proudly arching the canyon. Under its north end abutments, a shallow earthen shelf jutted forth and then fell one hundred feet down to the creek bed. Some earlier citizen of the highway had abandoned a partial bedframe with the springs intact on the ledge. This made for a perfect fire pit and grill.

Paul and I hitched through here. We liked these hills, this community of experimental artists. We asked the local Sheriff John, "Where can we camp?" He advised us that the land under bridges was public property and we'd be safe there. Sure enough, we were safe from the law. But maybe not so safe from the elements, local landowners, gravity, or the sprits that wail forth in the dark of the night in these Big Sur canyons. My camping experience was limited to my back yard and a few Girl Scout forays in designated campgrounds. My year-long tenure in

No Sleep Tonight: Hot Springs Canyon 1967

Haight Ashbury and my freewheeling anti-establishment philosophy qualified me as a hippie. We didn't even have a tent.

Paul got a gig at Esalen. He knew people. I came with him, riding his shadow. We needed a place to eat, we needed a place to roll out our bedroll. We peered at the Hot Springs Creek bridge and started hiking upward. In our knapsack we had a sooty cooking pot, a glass jug of water, the ubiquitous grainy brown rice, cheese, nuts, a few purloined chard leaves, and a small amount of marijuana. Paul's fellow work mate, Steve, came with us. Steve was just back from a Peace Corps stint in India, and he brought a small carton of plain yogurt in his pack to add to the rice. He also brought chocolate. Rick the guitar player parked his van at the end of the bridge and hiked down. We were set to cook dinner.

Fire was a problem. Too much smoke would give us away even in this twilight. We gathered a small bundle of twigs, added the brown shopping bag as starter fuel, and within minutes we had a small campfire. I lay a piece of the derelict bed springs over it, creating a tippy grill. I poured the water in the pot, added the rice, and we lit our pipe to wait for the entrée. Around us lay the remnants of bridge construction: old cement blocks, bare dirt, gravel. It wasn't pretty. Tires rumbled over our heads as an occasional truck made its way south. But the bubbling rice and the added chard smelled promising. We could do this. As the sole woman, I was the cook. I stirred the rice to ensure it would not stick to the pot. In the process, I overturned the carefully balanced pot set on the box springs, and the water gushed onto the fire, creating clouds of steam. Luckily the rice stayed in the pot. But now we needed water.

The only solution was to hike back down to the creek, many fathoms below. My fault, my job. I inched my way carefully in my slick leather-soled sandals. Once in the creek bed, I sank the glass jug into the stream and captured the cold water. I repositioned the jug and glanced up, gazing into the innards of the old bridge. Bats! Lots of them, lined the bridge supports. Startled, I instinctively combed my fingers through my hair to be sure none were clinging to me. I hastily marched my 22-year-old body back up that hill, hoping nothing was riding on my neck. "Bats!" I exclaimed to Paul, pointing downward. He laughed and spread out his arms.

"I'll get 'em," he responded, pretending to fly with a swooping motion. I giggled and pointed at his lopsided wings, and that was that. Another fear jettisoned. I added more water to the pot, and soon our fragrant rice, with yogurt and chard, was ready. Something about the open air, the fire, our new camaraderie, and the shared secret of this place, made the meal extra tasty. Or maybe it was the marijuana.

Bright stars appeared over the ocean, the creek roared, and the Pacific surf echoed up the canyon. Overhead an occasional car light flashed and we felt the wheels rumble, headed for the South Coast. Rick picked up his guitar. "Have you heard this? *Suzanne, take me down, to a place by the water...*" and we stepped into the myth.

Did I sleep under a bridge? Maybe for a minute. We spread out our bedroll on the ledge. I peed in the bushes, brushed my teeth by the light of the dwindling fire, swallowed my birth control pill and climbed into "bed". Paul and I were new lovers, so every night brought new discoveries, new places to nibble, professions of wonder and love, and new bruises from sleeping on the rough ground with its occasional rocky upcropping. Passion can be painful. Hot springs canyon proved to be a new challenge. The ground didn't have that soft sponge of soil; it was hard raw dirt with rocks. We dozed off, my sleep intermittently interrupted by an old truck rattling overhead. An hour later, I awoke, far from the blankets. I had slid down the hill and couldn't see to get back to the ledge. "Paul!" I squealed, alarmed. He hummed sleepily. I oriented to his voice and crawled back up, setting off pebbles that rolled out of hearing. Once again, we settled into slumber, only to repeat the downhill roll. I learned to cling to the hillside, and not let deep sleep intrude.

Just before drawn, the fog drifted in, floating its deep blanket up the canyon. Our outer quilt dampened, and I gave up on getting any more rest. This wouldn't work at all. I sourly gazed at Paul for having this dumb idea. My frown must have woken him.

He laughed and gathered the bedroll. "Shake it up. If we move fast, we can slip into Esalen for morning coffee before the seminarians fill up the lodge. Let's go." I didn't even get a minute to pull the leaves out of my hair. We never slept another night beneath the bridge.

As I became more familiar with this place, this jutting strip of level land west of Route One called Big Sur Hot Springs and renamed Esalen, I got to know the canyon. I tried to ignore my fear. I pretended I hadn't heard the stories of the wailing, the shrieks in the night. I heard gun shots sometimes. Hunters? I heard the drumbeats from the cabin back there, and I pretended it was common to hear drums all night. I didn't know about the heroin that led a few months later to the death of this drummer by overdose. On today's hike, Paul took off like a goat up the canyon paths, and I followed in my NYC handmade sandals, much more carefully, as I dodged the root balustrades nourishing the towering redwoods overhead. When a log crossed high over the creek, he took my hand loosely in support and led me over to the south face of the canyon. I made the mistake of looking down through the rushing waters at the haphazard splay of speckled rocks strewn below. My heart beat faster. I was terrified of falling, crashing onto these stones. There was darkness here, something I could feel in my bones, something about life and death and the forces that shape us, primordial and ancient, before God and redemption came along.

Dick Price, Esalen's co-founder, loved these canyons. He hiked daily into Hot Springs Canyon, as if its darkness called to him. The gestalt practice he learned from Fritz invited participants to become present to their darker shrouded issues, give them voice, and listen. In the process, change happened, unbidden. Dick helped us decipher these emotional minefields within, welcoming our dark side as it emerged into light, guiding us to use these new-found resources. Many years later, after an autumnal hike up into the watershed of the Rat Creek Fire, he would exclaim to me, "The canyon's all coming back. Everything is growing…" A month later, he was dead, killed at age fifty-five by a tumbling rock in this very canyon, just a few hundred yards further back. The wildfire's heat had shifted the earth and destabilized the boulder that gouged his skull and killed him instantly. Although deeply saddened, I wasn't surprised. I had met the Hot Springs Canyon spirits, the heavy death and reincarnation energy as well as its spritely new grown green ferns and spring sorrel. The redwoods, though, took first prize.

Those canyon redwoods drew from sources of decay, old civilizations. They sucked up hundreds of gallons of water daily to rise their spires toward the heavens. A favorite solitary pastime of mine was to lie on the canyon duff and look up. From this perspective, the tree rose forever like Jack's beanstock. Fire had ravaged these canyons regularly, leaving these conifers standing and flourishing, yet hollow. The burnt-out redwood trees created inner caves. These blacked hollow shelters were home for wintering Essalen tribes, nomads who left very few artifacts. Modern seekers and playful children camped in them now.

I camped here. I cooked here, hot rice topped with a spoonful of yogurt inspired by India, looked eastward from the West, as Walt Whitman extolled in *Passage to India*, "Tying the Eastern and Western Seas." My spirit found a way out of the quagmire of war and Vietnam and race and materialism into a place of peace, and sensuality, alert to the many levels of human consciousness. Living in theses canyons dropped me into a profound state of earth consciousness; I tolerated darkness as well the morning dawn. It was a place to retreat. Later I would choose to live above the canyon, in a spot more aligned with sunlight and an expanded view. As the canyons ascend, the rocky outcroppings on the hills watched over the coastline like ancient Gods positioned to monitor the pathway of mankind, the Barbary pirates, human greed and potentiality.

I didn't tell all this to these three women. I didn't need to. We'd lived it together.

I ended my story about the bridge and its canyon and emptied my wine glass. We friends sat quietly with the fire burning low. The bottle emptied. This Inn had served up meals for wanderers and offered locals birthday specials since the 30's when Route One ended here. Old chipped pitchers lined the wall, function turned into art. Shadows from the flames danced around us.

Route One had created this place to provide a resting stop at the end of the road. Route One also provided the plot line for my opening move into Big Sur.

The Number One Route Home

I had one foot in our Esalen hideout. But I still had our room on San Francisco's Duboce Street in a shabby two-story rooming house, cohabiting with a young Catholic University student, a dropped-out priest, a pregnant single woman, a professional photographer, and two women friends. My husband was out of town with his new girlfriend. My phone lived in our bedroom, along with a copy of the *San Francisco Oracle*, a small radio tuned to Otis Redding, and our single mattress on the floor. This was my fueling station and launch pad into the journey, a journey that could only occur on Route One, the Great Highway, the solo road into the Big Sur wilderness. Route One tracked the whole California Coastline, but I only knew my Route One, the pathway from the San Francisco sand dunes to Esalen's driveway. I journeyed back and forth. On this foggy morning, I had already hitched to the San Francisco shoreline and now confronted this great Cabrillo Highway, Route One.

I felt it as much as saw it. Solid, unending, flat here, rising there, bordered with sand and sage. A whiff of toxic petrol, a whiff of enticement. The breeze caught my hair, streaming out blond refractions. My chin lifted and a smile tickled the corners of my mouth. I could do this. I scratched at a grain of sand that had embedded itself in my eye. To the North I saw the band of gray as it curved past Cliff House by the old Sutro baths and dropped down toward the sea, following the coastline. To the south I saw clumps of seagrass and an occasional bright ribbon of reflected pavement. In front of me the blowing sand spun ridges across the road, reminding me that in California the earth doesn't stay in one place. Beyond the dunes lay the Pacific.

The Number One Route Home

Facing Northward toward San Francisco, I stuck out my thumb, pointing downstream Route One. I smiled into the oncoming traffic. This slippery roadbed was my dependable promise, my way into unimagined possibilities, my way back to Paul's arms. Today I would follow its serpentine roadway through the Pacifica Tunnel, wind above the remains of WW II bunkers hewn into the cliffs and pass the junction of Route One and Mission, Santa Cruz. I always straightened up at this tough intersection because I knew Route One could also be bloody. Recently a hitchhiker had been murdered in the Santa Cruz Mountains. I shifted my duffle bag, my thumb still extended. I wanted to get to Big Sur tonight.

Traffic was slow, I concluded, after 10 minutes and still no ride. Mostly American-made Fords and Chevys lumbered by, with an occasional contractor's truck or a delivery van filled with that famous sourdough bread. Out here on the coast, the VW bus consummated the ultimate promise of Route One: freedom, no rent, and a sweetheart to cuddle with at sunset time. An old woody with a surfboard atop drove past. Just behind me, I heard a car screech to a halt. A maroon Chevy, old and beat up, caught the curb and yelled out, "I'm going to Monterey. Want a ride?" I raced to the car and then checked him out. Just one guy, youngish. He looked ok. No dog in the back seat. No weird shit on the dashboard. No bare-breasted hula dancer mounted up front. Slightly fuzzy beard. "Yeah." I said, "Great." I never said where I was going. I wanted to be able to jump out at any time. Hitchhiking had its own guidebook. He smiled and tossed his backpack into the back seat, clearing the passenger seat for me. His car looked clean, and he did too. This'll do. I jumped in.

We fell under the serpent's influence as the road followed the coast, dipping down into riverbeds and rising into the pumpkin fields. With a single gas stop, where I chipped in my three dollars, we were soon in Monterey. He drove a bit further and dropped me off in Carmel at Ocean Avenue and Route One. Here the traffic toned up: more convertibles, a Porsche, the crazy car collector's old Cadillac. Route One was now an intersection more than a throughway. On the Monterey Peninsula, it was virtually the only easy way to get from place to place. A green VW bug swung wide to the shoulder and hailed me. Yes. Desperate now, I wanted a ride to get me south before dark. This time it was a couple, she with curly dark hair and dancing eyes and he with a cigarette in his mouth. Big Sur? No problem. They had a campsite at Willow Creek, so I was on their way.

I sat in the back seat, sometimes looking far out at the horizon and sometimes closing my eyes when the drop down to the sea was just too deep to fathom. Last week a car had gone off near Hurricane point. When they swung equipment down to find it, they found another rusted-out car body nearby. This big landscape stretched my life into a perspective of life, blood, and death. Faced with this reality, I chose to live more broadly, no more nine-to-five to support what I deemed to be an industrial military complex. Below, I could see the currents from the south sweep the ocean in shades of blues and greens, tipped with white-capped waves. I had the big view.

Again, the road swept us up, then plunged us under its spell as sunset blazed over the Pacific, firing up the waves to a frothy pink. The driver rested his arm on the seatback and ran his fingers through her curls. She shifted toward him, swinging her head in his direction. The hills caught the glow, and even the road ahead seemed rose colored. This pathway of asphalt could take us from the tip of the Pacific Northwest through the rocky Oregon Coast, the dippy California midlands and then smog out in LA only to emerge in Torrey Pines and Southern California for the surfers and the Navy boys. It promised fun, it promised getting away from today, it promised community, my lover's embrace, and something bigger than me. I never stepped foot on Route One without cheering up. It promised a new journey, every day. As a hitchhiker, I didn't even need to decide which way, north or south. If no rides came the way I originally set out to travel, I just turned around and tried the opposite direction. It never failed. I felt the charge and rose to meet it.

And that was the thing. Route One never failed me, and it never will. Even when it closes for a year at a time, even when a whole mountain lands on it, I know that the road is still there, the passageway between Canada and Mexico, all the while bound by the Pacific breakers and the westerly mountains' rise. If it closes due to mud, we will walk around, walk over hills and ford swollen creeks. Sooner or later, we will step foot on it again; it will wait for us, wait to take us to the next interesting bend. It never says stop. It tempts the bridegroom, cheers the depressed, taunts the gold digger. For me, the hitchhiker, I now knew beyond doubt that the world changes daily depending on the sands and rains and constellations over Route One. Yet the bedrock of this planet beneath this lazy old road carved out by convicts in the nineteen-thirties holds firm and flexible.

"Right here," I called out to the driver as the Hot Springs sign came into view. "Here's my stop." If I hustled, I'd still make it to the lodge deck before dark. Paul should be nearby. Would he be glad to see me? Or would some other refugee off Route One be on his mind or worse, in his arms? That thought didn't feel good. I stood up straight, shook out my hair, and strode down the hill to meet this love story—be it the man, the place, or the pure pleasure of it all. I heard the drums in the distance, and a singer joined in.

"Hey!" A waved hand surprised my reverie. Paul caught my shoulder and spun me toward him. "Missed you," he murmured, tickling me as he held me close. "I saved you some dinner. Then we can take a bath."

My First Bath

I don't like baths. Getting stuck for half an hour in a small, tiled tub enclosure with tepid or too hot water is an experience I'd rather avoid. So, on that starry night when Paul asked me if I wanted to take a bath, I shook my head, no. Then I noticed several people strolled by, carrying towels, and heading down a steep dirt path, seemingly into the sea. What was this?

I should have paid more attention. The sign at the entryway to Esalen still read "Big Sur Hot Springs". But I'd never visited a hot springs, or an open bathhouse. I hadn't been on a path like this one, either, hugging the cliffside. We seemingly walked downward for hundreds of feet, with no lights to guide our way. I could hear the surf on my right, giving me my bearings. Soon a faint light appeared in front on me, a bare electric light bulb dangling at the bathhouse entrance. I breathed a sigh of relief to reach this manmade footing, and the last few steps. I could hang my clothes here, or…. wait, no clothes in a strange place? I stopped, I didn't know what to think. Paul jauntily walked straight forward. I followed, peering into every shadowy corner. A few more steps down and I was met with the unpleasant stench of sulfur. It reminded me that my brother hated the smell of hard-boiled eggs, this same smell. I heard lapping, gurgling, smelly, splashing water in every direction. Neptune's Cave.

By the light of four burning candles, I could dimly make out two square cement tubs, each big enough to accommodate six people easily. I'd be bathing with other people, too. What next? Between tubs I saw two ordinary iron-footed bathtubs. Luckily it was late enough now that we shared the big tub with only one other bather. I shed my clothes, carefully hanging them on the wooden pegs so that I could relocate them. Naked! Paul had nabbed one towel for the both of us, so in my complete birthday suit I stepped into the water. We joined the lone bather, a quiet man who said little. He seemed stoned.

That's when I learned what all the fuss was about, why hot springs are revered around the world, why the original word root for spa means healing water, why health insurance in Europe pays your way into a hot springs when you are sick. I trailed my fingers into the pool. This water was hot! Paul submerged himself in the heat and then sprang from the large hot tub into the iron tub next to it filled with cold water. "Hey, try this," he encouraged. No way! I gingerly slid into the bath, getting used to the warmth. I settled into a seated position, legs outstretched, water up to my chin. I exhaled deeply, and then noticed I was inexplicably buoyant. I took another slow breath and invited this water to float my arms on the surface. My whole body soon followed. I felt light and yet completely wrapped in the spring's warm embrace. Soon Paul was embracing me too in this slippery-smooth bath.

My skin flushed and I swung my legs out of the deep tub and into the cool evening. I wiped my face with my half of the bath towel and then lay prone on one of the narrow pine tables scattered around the bathhouse. Stars spread overhead. I could feel rather than see the deep oceanic horizon and cliffs reaching to the north and south, a space extending beyond borders. Paul took a final cold plunge and stood over me, dripping chilly water onto my back in a not unpleasant way. "Stop!" I squealed as I scooted over, careful to avoid splinters, and he joined me on the benchlike table. The Pacific hit the rocks below, releasing fine mist that rose up to us. All my neural circuits found new pathways, stimulated by the sea sound and calmed by the waters. The tingly result called me to "wake up!" to myself. It also left me so relaxed that I could barely lift my feet to walk back up that hill. I wanted a few hours of sleep before dawn.

Did Dick Price Run by Here?

Paul hoisted the floppy bedroll onto his shoulder, and we walked silently through the dark, feeling our way down the dusty back road to our newly claimed campsite. We'd explored the area carefully last week and happened upon a small level clearing in the bushes a quarter mile north of hot springs creek. While I was working in the city, Paul tugged out the dead brush and monkeyweed and swept down the dirt. He knew how to make a patch into a home.

Our new domicile lay where no one would look, behind a hedge of fragrant sage and low-lying chaparral framed by fallen eucalyptus branches. This was private property, and what's more, a nearby resident in the Art Barn guarded the neighborhood with bulldog ferocity. I carried my duffle and the canvas food bag. "Quiet!" Paul breathed near my ear as the trail flattened on the northern reach of the back road. I looked at him quizzically. Where was it? After carefully checking both directions for nighttime strollers, he led me in an awkward scramble up a small crumbling dirt embankment, then swept aside the sage branches for another dozen feet. Home. Brushing the leafy debris out of my clothes would become part of the daily ritual. I entered the space slowly. Paul flung aside a downed branch and pulled up a few errant monkeyweed plants to make space for our bedroll. I inhaled the spicy scented night air. Perhaps I would be the first to ever sleep on this virgin land, I smiled to myself. I chose to ignore the hand-built hut that lay out of sight just south of us, and the small clapboard house with its peeling white paint on the other side of the road. A four-foot-high granite rock to the east would mark our headboard. This was ours. Paul rolled out the bedroll, fluffed the pillows against the stone and gave it a trial run. "Feels flat to me," he pronounced. I didn't notice the lumps until later. After the hot bath, I was asleep in a minute.

Exiting into the daylight required gut feeling and attentive listening. The moment I sprang out of the overgrown bushes, I would be totally visible to anyone strolling by. I didn't know what would happen if I got caught, but I guessed it meant expulsion from this place where I wanted to be.

After a couple of near misses, I became aware of a slender dark-haired man who often walked by quickly heading north, seemingly without schedule. With his eyes focused straight ahead, chin tucked down, tanned legs stretching out beneath drab shorts, he kept a fast, determined pace. His short hair and clean-shaven face indicated he wasn't a pothead, while his worn-down running shoes set him apart from the well-heeled Esalen guests. In this community there weren't many people in the middle; either you were rich and probably from LA or you were living the hand-to-mouth hippie artist lifestyle. At other times of day, he walked by dressed in a crumpled green plaid short-sleeved shirt and slacks, apparently going somewhere. Luckily, I always caught a glimpse of him just before my descent down the embankment. I was certain he hadn't seen me.

Paul's work shift at the gate ended at 2 pm. "Hey, let's go," he called as he headed up the steep Esalen hill. This short sharp incline was a painful experience for my already tight leg muscles, but I followed my usual ten feet behind, trying to be more enthusiastic about climbing yet another Big Sur hillside. I was panting at the top and stopped long enough to catch my breath.

"C'mon!" chided Paul, turning away and heading north on Route One. Not one to stand still when he hitch-hiked, he set out walking in the direction he was headed, swinging his uplifted thumb wide to the side. "Keep moving," he admonished me. When I saw him in silhouette, his legs seemed extra long. We walked over the bridge and peered downward into the gulp of Hot Springs Canyon. Who's sleeping there tonight? I wondered. Good luck to them! As we stepped off the bridge onto the roadbed, I glimpsed that same dark-haired man, now headed toward us. He had jogged along the back road and then cut back south where it joined Route One. Once over the bridge, he could complete the loop by walking fast down the very hill we had just marched up.

He nodded to Paul and almost smiled at me. Paul responded with "Hey!" and a small salute of recognition.

"Do you know who that was?" I asked, watching the dark-haired man trot down the highway, curious that Paul's manner was ever so slightly formal.

"Oh, that's Dick Price," responded Paul brightly. "I've heard he's in charge here, but I don't see it." Paul shrugged his shoulders. "Seems like a nice guy. Kind of a loner." He repositioned his outstretched thumb and the next car, a newish light blue Ford sedan driven by a couple of sightseers, picked us up and took us to Nepenthe for our afternoon hangout on the deck.

We never bought the restaurant's dollar a cup coffee or a beer. Instead, we sat on the cement benches above the deck and watched the parade of tourists who spent a day travelling to get here and hoped to get to Carmel tonight. "There's Kim Novak," pointed out Paul, leaning forward. A famed movie star, she strolled in the midst of a gaily dressed group. I could hear her laughing in that breathy way I remembered from the silver screen. No one paid her any extra attention. Hollywood denizens came here to escape the bright lights and then were disappointed when they weren't noticed. If we stayed late enough, we would listen in on the local old-timers like Walter Trotter as they gathered around the fire pit and rehashed their day and the antics of their bulldozer or new wife. Those long winter evenings honed their storytelling skills. Sometimes Henry Miller joined from the side.

"Hey, let's hit the road," Paul interrupted my people-watching. I stood up, tugging my short dress down. We descended the winding pathway between scarlet geraniums, the old-style green phone booth, and a full array of densely planted succulents. As the sun set into the Pacific, we cruised back to Esalen in the bed of a gray Chevy pick-up. "Poor man's sports car." The wind gaily whipped my hair on this warm summer night riding down Route One.

Paul pulled the graveyard shift on the gate a few days later. We star-gazed all night, dazzled by the brightest stars I'd ever seen. We spotted one, brighter, that seemed to be moving on its own track. I initially caught sight of it on the southeastern horizon, just over the mountains. Slowly it climbed the sky. Paul voiced his invitation for a flying saucer landing. He waved his arms invitingly and danced around, "C'mon in!" I hoped this wasn't it. I tracked the bright light's path. Sure enough, the other stars were climbing the heavens, too, but on a slower path. I anxiously pointed this out to Paul. "Yeah, that's the movement of the universe." He scrutinized the bright light that now emitted an occasional blink. "Hmmm. Must be one of those new satellites."

As a result of this all-nighter, we slept late the next morning. I dressed, careful not to get leaves inside my cotton dress, and Paul rolled up the bedroll. To someone even a few feet away, our site was completely invisible. We dropped a fallen eucalyptus branch over our mound of stuff to complete our camouflage. Paul grabbed his towel and slid down the embankment first, with me right on his heel. At exactly the same moment, Dick Price ran right in front of us. We stopped front, center, and present with absolutely no way to explain our sudden appearance. He slowed down and smiled toward Paul. "Oh, got a camp in there?" looking uphill toward our camp. He kept jogging forward. "You work the gate, don't you? Good!" thereby bestowing his blessings. He shared not a word of our hideaway to anyone else.

People seeking admission through the Esalen gate mentioned Dick, too, casually letting the guard know that they were his guests. When Paul sent me to check, Dick glanced up, surprised, then nine times out of ten he waved them in. An hour later as I filled my coffee mug in the lodge, I spotted him huddled in conversation with a tableful of professorial looking men. He sat with attention, his posture forward, chin resting in his hand, listening. He inserted a question, and the middle man sat up, pleased. Dick sat another minute, waved his good-byes, and hurried off.

I finished my hot coffee outside the lodge seated on the thick bench by the pay phone. He passed by again with loose papers in his hand, bound for the back office. I learned he wrote to these luminaries of the times—Abe Maslow, Will Schultz, Virginia Satir—and slotted them into the schedule of events, working with Esalen co-founder Michael Murphy. Almost overnight the Institute had gained a reputation for cutting edge seminars.

As Dick ducked through the back entrance into the Esalen office, I realized I had never once seen him walking slowly or resting into the peaceful drop of the sunset. Where was his bedroom, or his bed? Late that night, an attractive blonde woman named Jane pulled up to the gate and asked for him. I didn't know where to start looking. I checked the office cubbyhole where he was last seen. No, not there. In his inimitable style he appeared three minutes later. I too would come to rely on my intuition.

Dick experimented with the paranormal and with humanistic psychology. Like Fritz Perls, his mentor who he invited to live and work at Esalen, he was most interested in today, the present moment of experience. Unpacking family history held little interest for him, nor did any particular spiritual encampment. He didn't do a lot of talking about things—elephant shit, Fritz called it—but chose to address issues directly in present time enactment. I spotted him in a myriad of places: a Berkeley apartment where he lost his entry key and climbed through the bathroom window to the surprise of me and my boyfriend; at Muktananda's darshan and talk in Berkeley awaiting the peacock feather blessing on the head; on a solo walk deep into Hot Springs Canyon, where this time he was the trespasser. "Nobody captures the flag." He declared.

Fritz, the old, bearded guy in the gray jumpsuit who hung out in the lodge, started leading a monthlong psychological seminar with several noted shrinks and psychologists in attendance, including Esalen Board member Jack Downing. Gestalt therapy was new, immediate. It fit the times and made common sense. It debunked introspection and philosophizing. "And how do you feel now?" Fritz drew on group members to enact rather than explain. These exercises arose out of his early participation in psychodrama. His gestalt group "show me" method of work brought the point home with real emotional effect. The in-the-moment dialog went deep and drew tears, regrets, reconciliations.

I sometimes saw Dick walking fast toward the class, posture forward, head tucked down. Later I saw him sitting in Perls' meeting room, watching Fritz intently as Fritz in turn watched the couple in front of him. Clearly, they had come to him for help. He hadn't said much, just "Do you hear what she is saying?" and "What is your expectation?" Then looking at the rest of the group, "It is your expectation that is the problem."

I would later learn that Dick came from a family with great expectations for him, expectations that didn't match up with his personality. His father forced him to quit a short but intense love relationship. Dick ended up in a mental hospital with a diagnosis of depression. He received the latest innovative treatment, electric shock therapy, to jumpstart his brain back from the dark mood that had taken over. It didn't work and Dick learned how to demand his release. Now ten years later, he felt comfortable enough with Fritz to undertake opening into his intense personal history. "We all have our dark canyons," a fellow seminar member explained. Even in the group, one barely noticed Dick. He played the outsider even as he was a key player at the Institute. If I needed to talk to him, I caught up with him at the baths.

As the Institute's fame grew, a man phoned Esalen's front desk to crisply request admission into the leaders' training program. I asked Dick about this. "Your personal growth and participation in the group *is* your leadership training," he responded, favoring a "bottoms up" philosophy rather than coursework to create inexperienced experts. He took his gestalt studies seriously and occasionally joined in with Fritz as he openly guided one of his students.

Years later as a gestalt facilitator he would borrow a quote from Richard Bach, "We all teach what we most need to learn" and add, "And we are all our own worst students."

While Dick was very much on site, his co-founder, Michael Murphy, kept his home in Marin County, over the Golden Gate Bridge. I didn't meet Michael for months. A big dreamer, he was creating an urban Esalen site, 1776 Union Street, San Francisco. Michael carried the programing inspiration for Esalen, and Dick added the teachers he wanted. Both men valued concepts sourced in Asia. Both cared passionately about expanding human capacity, with an "anything goes" openness. The two old friends who had met at Stanford agreed to disagree about the focus of Esalen programs and this tension added vitality to the curriculum. Some said it was Michael's land and Dick's money that allowed the place to tick.

Michael leaned toward the world of ideas, philosophy, meditation and the insights gleaned during his year at the Aurobindo Ashram in Pondicherry. His deep green V-neck sweater and preppy style aligned with his golfing passion. I didn't see much of him my first year.

Dick championed psychology and personal experience, "Where do you feel that?" inquiries. He sought courses you could wrap your hands around, psychology that invoked awareness and choice rather than understanding. He invited pioneer bodyworkers like Ida Rolf to come and teach their method. He offered his body as a prime subject on their tables. I jumped onto her student's table at first chance. The notion that emotions lay locked in the body made sense to me. As I walked across the room I recalled my father's limp from early aged polio, and I noticed I limped, too, in identifying with him. My limp was gone when I carefully rolled off the table an hour later.

Virginia Satir kept a small cabin on the top row of Esalen's motel housing. She seemed part of their team somehow. I'm not sure if it was her size or her command of space that made her loom so big to me. Her broad body, draped wool poncho, and loud voice carried authority. Her book, *Conjoint Family Therapy*, came out a few years earlier and I puzzled over the title. What did conjoint mean? I'd never heard of family therapy before I met her, never thought of looking at the system rather than the defining problem child. Somehow this linked to my experience as a social worker in the Bedford Stuyvesant neighborhood, New York City. Clearly this poverty-riddled population flailed because of hopeless economic pressures on their family systems. Like me, and many of those at the Institute, Virginia posited the belief that mental shifts resulted in enhanced self-esteem. As Fritz said, self-regulation could lead to political change and peace. This was the inside-out change I sought in early SDS political meetings back at Rutgers. I understood now why I had to leave the Berkeley rallies behind when they started yelling, "Kill the pigs." Changing the culture would come from the inside, not through slogans.

Was this the remedy I sought? Those political movements were great at raising issues, but not at long term solutions. Changing the system at the individual's level and then working to communicate person-to-person made a lot more sense to me. But—how to talk directly? This was my challenging piece, breaking all the old nice girl rules.

Occasionally I joined the small team that dutifully cleaned Virginia's cabin before and after each arrival. "You're a placater," she called out to me one day when I hid my disgruntlement at cleaning the refrigerator with an offer to get her coffee. Huh? I soon learned she grouped dialog into five styles: placating, blaming, computing, distracting, and congruent communication. I couldn't help but notice that only one of those – congruent – meant actually listening without a lot of pre-conceived filters. I certainly knew how to blame! I could placate. Just listening and taking in what I heard without embroidering it with my own spin meant climbing onto somebody else's wavelength. I tried it out, feeling stupid, and within ten minutes I had a new friend in this community.

Virginia came and went on her own schedule. I learned she was one of the signers in Esalen's non-profit articles of incorporation, the legal entity that got this place going. "Virginia's here!" stirred the staff to action. Her fame grew as her book sold its heretical idea that the solution lay not in one person but the system and context. Blame didn't help. Like Fritz, she emphasized the unique potential of each person. I walked out of her cabin and looked to the drummer on the edge of the cliff to my left and the curly blonde-haired gardener intent of planting a rosebush on my right. Yup, this was the right place to be different. What about me? Was I still always trying to please – placate- rather than express?

FALL 1965 SEMINARS at Big Sur Hot Springs
sponsored by Esalen Institute

Within a single lifetime, our physical environment has been changed almost beyond recognition. But there has been little corresponding change in how we, as individuals, relate to the world and experience reality. Such a change is inevitable, however — indeed, it is imminent. New tools and techniques of the human potentiality — generally unknown to the public and to much of the intellectual community — are already at hand; many more are presently under development. We stand on an exhilarating and dangerous frontier, — and must answer anew the old questions: "What are the limits of human ability, the boundaries of the human experience? What does it mean to be a human being?"

This fall, the Esalen Institute presents a series of seminars led by some of the pioneers along the frontiers of human development. These men represent widely varying approaches — from the scientific shaping of human behavior to the temporal uses of religion and mysticism, from innovation in education to the exploration of extrasensory perception. All of them share a common concern with human change and mankind's ultimate destination.

Date	Seminar Leader
August 27-29	Rollo May
September 10-12	Bishop James A. Pike and Alan Watts
September 17-19	Gardner Murphy
October 1-3	Carl Rogers
* October 3-6	Richard E. Farson
October 8-10	B. F. Skinner and Jerome I. Berlin
* October 10-15	Jerome I. Berlin
October 15-17	Sidney Cohen
October 22-24	Maurice Friedman
October 29-31	Frank Barron
* October 31-November 5	George I. Brown
November 5-7	Donald D. Jackson and Virginia Satir
* November 7-12	Virginia Satir
November 12-14	Sidney Jourard and Gerald Goodman
* November 14-17	Gerald Goodman
November 19-21	J. B. Rhine
November 26-28	Clark Moustakas and Hobart Thomas
December 3-5	S. I. Hayakawa
December 10-12	Robert Gerard
December 10-12	J. F. T. Bugental

* workshops

No More Nice Girl

A new catalog of events emerged quarterly as Dick and Michael, urged on by Virginia, enthusiastically drilled down on Esalen's mission, to discover and develop the hidden potential that lies within each of us. The ideas were radical, I was young, and so was the faculty, mostly under forty years old. One dynamic bioenergetics "Radex" group leader was a spritely twenty-seven-year-old woman from New Jersey. Her long hair framed her face as she directed this week's seminar. With an earnest unsmiling demeanor, she suggested we could unlock our hidden energy blocks within our body. Here was that idea again, that we free the mind through the body rather than the other way around. I leaned forward to listen. She directed us to lie on our backs with knees bent and feet on the floor, extolled us to relax, to breath deep, letting out a small sound as we exhaled through our mouth. Lying down felt good on this carpeted floor. Yet soon I was oddly unsettled, fidgety. She bent over me and gently touched my shoulder, then grasped my feet and encouraged me, "push your legs straight into my hands." The next minute, tears that had long laid dormant – I hadn't cried in five years - rolled down my face. At first my flooded eyes and jerky gulps of breath felt scary, evoking a childlike sorrow and sense of fragility, but with each sob I felt my chest expand as my ribs widened.

I wasn't the only one crying; most of the other people in the room expressed jagged breathes, sobs, and wiped tears away. Sound rose and fell in the meeting room and finally the assistants passed out Kleenex. With our leader's guidance, my shaky emotions transformed into a resource rather than a liability. We learned to welcome this damp up-swelling rather than quickly swallowing it away. "What do those tears want to say?" she directed me to ask myself. I sure didn't know. I just knew there were places inside me that longed to get out, no matter how messy. Fifteen minutes later, my eyes felt clearer than they had in years, and my mouth softened into a smile.

Dick's focus was his own healing, and this appealed to me. My stint in the anti-war movement during college and in New York opened my eyes to my compatriots' contentious nature even as we marched for peace. If we couldn't talk to each other, how could we talk to Russia? With this singular insight, I swept aside my social worker persona—focused outwardly on helping others—and dove inward to confront my own ingested family expectations and inhabitations. Life wasn't all about being a nice girl. With chin held high, I defiantly chose to bed down with this wayfaring actor in this lumpy campsite. Still, I found it hard to talk about, identify, or usually even find my own feelings. I didn't have the map for this territory. I just knew the territory existed.

Dick was unwinding the trauma of the electric jolts he'd received as his alleged treatment for depression. He threw off the bonds of corporate familial correctness. I could see the change in his jawline as his face relaxed and his tightly sprung shoulders began to flex. He sampled every workshop that came through Esalen.

The following year he assumed the gestalt mantle after Fritz Perls grew tired of the U.S.'s warmongering politics and moved to Vancouver Island, Canada, to establish Cowachan, a loose community of gestalt practitioners. Dick visited him there, returning with egalitarian notions such as disbanding the massage crew. Everyone would give each other massages instead. The massage crew took a week off and then were hastily called back into service. Fritz died the following year and Dick seamlessly took over gestalt leadership at Esalen.

I sampled gestalt therapy in a staff group, eight of us gathered on the rug propped up randomly by oversized pillows. I sat stone-faced, acutely uncomfortable with the prospect of revealing myself, sure I would say the wrong thing, or fail to use the required 'I' statement. I tucked my elbows close to my chest protectively. The leader, a psychologist from the neighboring property, encouraged us to "check in." At his prodding. one chunky dark-haired young woman said emphatically, "I'm not here to work on old family stuff," and then a minute later screamed at her mother. Or rather, she screamed at the India print pillow that stood in for Mom. Screamed at her mother! I wasn't thinking much about my mother. I closed my eyes per the directions, "Just become aware of your body and any feelings today." My whole predicament loomed large. My loose-limbed relationship with Paul, coupled with my fuzzy separation from Bob, rose before me. I didn't want to see it. I wanted to avoid making any decision regarding this guy who I invited into my life. I didn't have answers to those "What am I doing here?" questions that writ large in the middle of the night. I said nothing in this first gestalt group.

Later I enrolled in a gestalt workshop led by Dick, whose low-toned manner overshadowed the psychologist co-leader. Pursuing my dream image, he led me to explore a police confrontation. "Do they look like anyone you know?" I looked and saw one of my strict Scandinavian relatives staring at me, now cast as a policeman. I laughed and never had the dream again.

I still didn't know where Dick lived. He built Esalen to provide a safe nest and invited local crazies and those in workshops to come and sit with him as they explored their own interior implosions. Firmly opposed to the use of medication to tone down depression, he smiled and sat in witness for those who were willing to mentally welcome their demons. He had no interest in "fixing" people, substituting the words "the rapist" for therapist. As one participant sat on the pillow and complained that he couldn't quit his job, Dick suggested, "Put the judge over there on the pillow. Is he far enough away? How does that feel in your body, to see the judge over there? (Pause) What do you want to say to him?" After the man blasted the judge, who now looked a lot like his uncle, Dick continued, "Now switch. Let the judge respond." Switch sides! Now I could see my predicament more lightly. Dick called his role "reflector" and let us take our own journey through our mind maze, calling us out when we spoke about ideas and plans rather than what was present right here. He sat calmly, no matter what we said or wherever he slept this month. He accepted our campsite, he accepted the crazy journalist with guns, and he didn't call the cops when one of the locals shot up the Esalen sign. His straightforwardness called forth unbidden foundational issues to come out of hiding.

We tragically lost him. He died from a rock blow to his skull while exploring the deep recesses of Hot Springs Canyon. This land and its sharp curves carved his blueprint for Esalen, liberating a space for our collective mind and full potentiality. Dick Price met us on the ground, accepted me as I was rather than what I stood for. My hostility toward the establishment, the industrial military complex and organized religion, found no holding place in his Esalen. He lived right here with us. Yet he was aloof by nature, definitely not the kind of guy I would engage in conversation at the Esalen bar. Michael would go on to write many books; Dick lived in the present and wrote down almost nothing on paper. Yet he inscribed indelible messages in my deep mental recesses.

Paul settled into his job on the Esalen gate, working the night shift. He bought leather boots and corduroy pants and a belt to hold them up. Someone gave him a scuffed leather aviator jacket for the cold nights. I, in turn, still hitched back and forth to San Francisco, sustaining myself as an office temp worker. More to the point, I still had a husband there (although he was out of town with, I think, his girlfriend) and we had a room on DuBose street. I swung back and forth between realities. When I walked Haight Street now, all I heard was talk, talk. I no longer engaged. I'd acted. I was smug in my convictions. I was living the dropped-out life they sought. After a quick visit, I scurried back to my new-found community down the coast.

The Esalen social territory was clearly mapped out into two groups. Theirs, the seminarians and faculty attending workshops, remained intellectually engaged in spirited conversation over half-empty dinner plates with their eyes wide and their legs crossed. They chatted brightly as they checked into their seminars and often looked intently at each other, deeply engaged. They drank mugs of coffee or bought a glass of wine or beer at the bar to enjoy in the candlelight. They seemed older.

Ours, the staff and hangers-on, aged seventeen to forty, sheltered among the bushes around the cliffside edge of the lawn or dined together at one long table by the back wall of the lodge. I counted myself as staff. When Paul worked, he got a meal and shared it with me. I shared my fig newtons. Most often we stayed outside, where Jack from the shop passed around a skinny rolled-up joint. No alcohol. We were living the dream; we'd dropped out; we knew that intellectual talk was just that. Talk. The seminarians sitting in the lodge dodged our mandate of giving it all up to strive toward full potential, to live for today rather than tomorrow's career. Even sanity was up for debate. I too went with the flow. If I lived for today, I didn't need to make any decisions about tomorrow.

Competition and Connection

I fished around inside my shoulder bag, feeling under my book, my wallet, and my glasses. A string of glass beads. Wads of paper. Where was it? Finally, I unearthed the plastic circular packet: my birth control pills, Enovid by brand name. I might be willing to give up a lot of 20th century trappings, but this one was important. I enjoyed the freedom to be with Paul without a future plan. This little packet made it all possible: no babies now. No need for a household. I turned the dial so that today's pill popped up and I swallowed it with a gulp. Done!

The blossoming fertility around me was unnerving. On the Esalen staff, Donna was obviously very pregnant, and her partner doted on her. Yet – as I heard it – this tiny miracle about to be born was not his child. Only a few days after my second visit, I heard the news: it's a boy! A second woman, Storm, continued to gain girth and looked lovelier by the day. Their child would surely be blessed.

Sweeping my hair out of my eyes, I straightened my posture and swung open the heavy redwood door to the lodge. I found a foursome of women enjoying a cup of coffee together at the middle table, drawing their heads close in and then exploding outward with laughter. For those in the established community of Esalen, I understood that women friends were a must. They hunkered down together in storms for weeks at a time. The income they gained from their crafts sales was uncertain; the kitchen shift varied according to the number of guests. They helped each other during lean periods and rejoiced at each other's good fortune. They had history. Their partners worked at the

Institute, and many had been on board since its founding in 1963. When this coterie of women took a glance over at my loose blonde hair, perky braless breasts, and the way my Greek shoulder bag slung freely off my shoulder, they drew closer together. "Another hippie slut!" they proclaimed under their breath, glancing at their partners at a nearby table. Or so I believed.

None of them reached out to me. When I shyly said hi to the dark-haired woman I'd met yesterday, she gave me a short "Hello!" in return and then continued her conversation, without further acknowledgement. I knew her through her pal, Kathy, a younger woman with doe-like eyes and a slender body. We'd discovered that she, too, was of Finnish descent. Kathy was younger, a waitress who occasionally baked delicious deserts. She sat next to me on the staff bench outside last week when we had tarot readings. While a free spirit at heart, she wasted no time letting me know that Ed, the morning breadmaker, was her old man. They lived in a small hand-built shack just north of our secret camping spot. Ed? Oh, right, he'd talked yesterday about Freud and falling for someone who wasn't available, or an affair.

"I get it," I said to him then. "I've often fallen for someone who was unavailable."

"It's because you and your mother were in competition for your father, "he explained, his reddish hair blending with his unshorn beard. "That's what Freud said, anyway," he added with a chuckle. He was a little older and he clearly wasn't trying to put one over on me. He challenged me to look at my family tangles. I shook off the suggestion.

Competition. We women, new and old, competed for jobs. We competed for housing. Yes, we competed for men. It was only through our relationship with a man that a female could truly win in this community. You had to shack up with someone to have a roof over your head. Sisterhood was out the window until you had an old man of your own. Taking it all to heart, I completely shunned the NY times woman assigned to write the inside story of this crazy new human potential movement. She was just a little too engaging. She asked Paul for one of his poems. He said yes, and that was it for me. "And how does she know you write

Steeped

poetry?" I demanded. When she asked again, he said he'd changed his mind.

The single link for me between staff and locals and work was the Stevens family, most notably Ellen. She and Ken had arrived last spring from Los Angeles and parked their homemade camper in the lodge lot. Ellen had a tow-haired toddler, Thane. My second day on property, she hit me up. "Hey, I've got the evening waitress shift tonight and Ken's doing dishes. Can you babysit for me? I'll sneak you out a dinner."

Fair enough. I watched Thane in the back of their home on wheels. Small shelves on one side held cookware and crackers; on the opposite side a faint onions aroma arose from the stored produce. Thane entertained himself by dashing from one side to the other, giggling when he banged the wall. We shared a sliced apple. "Pee!" he said suddenly. I opened the flap so he could gleefully urinate onto the dirt driveway. Moments later, Ellen eased her way in with a beer in one hand and my dinner plate balanced in the other. "Whew!" She exclaimed. "That old guy just couldn't keep his hands off. I told him that I noticed, and I'd sent my last husband to the hospital. That stopped him." We laughed as we shared a joint and she popped the top off a second beer. The story about her ex? It turned out to be true.

Ellen was my age, a college dropout from LA. She'd married young, and just as she said, she'd caught her husband cheating. When she confronted him, he hit her. She bided her time, then wacked him with a cast iron frying pan as he slept. She packed up Thane and left. Ken was an old friend who provided a safe haven, and here they were, lovers now, checking out Esalen. She stood taller than me, and her short hair and frayed bell bottoms spelled girl next door rather than hippie. Her shapeless tee shirt barely made it past her waist on her tall frame. Her movements weren't quite coordinated, as if her body wasn't all connected.

Her droll humor kept us all laughing. She focused on highlighting what was right in front of our eyes yet somehow missed. She told it like it was. Or rather, she told it like it was in her world. She wrote off a co-worker's grumpiness: "What's the matter? You didn't get laid last night?" She grudgingly took orders from the male cook. "So, you've got some old lettuce and you're trying to pass it off it?" she pronounced disparagingly. After listening in on last night's phone calls at the public pay phone, she deduced, "You're never too old to be somebody's sweet young thing." An apt observation, I came to learn. She often resembled the Tibetan Sherpa, who climbed the world's steepest mountains with determination and laughter. We might call this crazy wisdom.

Her partner, Ken, in contrast, was low voiced and thoughtful. He too opposed any sign of authority and made it a point to never advance himself beyond his dishwashing gig. He tied his long dark hair back and bent his youthful body over the stacks of greasy plates and pots. He practiced his yoga daily during staff hour at the baths. He seldom spoke up, although in one discussion where staff wanted reimbursement for the meals they didn't eat, He laughed and proclaimed, "Let them just eat dollar bills."

When the institute-wide firing came the following November, we were all canned and went different ways. Ken and Ellen moved into a campground up the road. "You gotta hear this," Ken said on our initial visit to their one-room cabin. He fired up his new battery phonograph on their porch under the redwoods and played the Beatles' *Sgt. Pepper's Lonely Heart's Club Band*. "What do you do when I sing out of tune, do you stand up and walk out on me? Oh, I get high with a little help from my friends..." they harmonized. "I get by with a little help from my friends..." I was just learning how deeply we could help each other.

Twenty years later, I looked up from my "Information" table at the local community college where I served as student counselor. "Can we join you to make more space?" a young man asked as he shoved another table over. I turned to my new table partner: Ellen.

"What's new with you?" she asked without missing a beat. "I'm onto this recovery stuff now." She held up a pamphlet for a local program. "I've been sober for five years." I looked at her, smiled in recognition of this important milestone. Sober, with her sense of humor intact, bent now on helping those whose intoxicants had tipped them over the edge. We shared a "Who'd have guessed?" chuckle, and then I referred the student in front of me to her desk. It takes a community.

Look, It's George Leonard

A few repeat workshop leaders caught onto us and hung out with the more colorful staff during their off hours. Esalen never failed to surprise me – after all, Joan Baez had LIVED here – yet nonetheless I was surprised when one of my longtime heroes offered me a ride back to San Francisco. He noticed me. Or, more precisely, he pointed me to one of his writers who was driving to North Beach that afternoon with room to spare. My ride. One thing you might not recall about me: I originally wanted to go into journalism. I edited high school and college newspapers. I majored in American culture in college. Truth, I was at Esalen because of my passion for communities as well as my appreciation for Alan Watts' books.

George Leonard edited the slick US weekly news magazine, a big splashy photo-filled treat titled simply *Look* that arrived in 2.9 million homes weekly. If I had known this lanky guy in front of me, interested in what I had to say about the afternoon sitar concert was THAT George Leonard, I would have been shy. Instead, I stepped up with a snappy response. Minutes later I wrote down something for him in my twisty left-handed fashion and he promptly pointed out that I wrote upside down. "That affects your brain," he pronounced. I took him at his word and challenged myself to orient my paper the other direction and write in a more comfortable fashion. I think my brain liked the shift.

George was friends with Michael Murphy, Esalen's co-founder. More than that, he saw this burgeoning culture around him for what it was: a vote for a life that was more natural, more honest in relationship, a deeper dive into personal awareness. Sex might be viewed as a sacred ritual à la the Kama Sutra teachings, rich with lingering sensuality, rather than a shameful back-alley dalliance or marital habit. He didn't short-shift people like Paul and me as free love slackers; he watched us closely. His saxophone had howled in his earlier years and now he listened to our funky guitar and drum music. He saw the embodied connection of our lifestyle with our world view. When Storm danced by in her flowing dress decorated with embroidered symbols, he paid attention to its intimate handmade look.

More than that, he wrote about it. Several issues of *Look* Magazine would be devoted to this phenomenon that I, too, was glimpsing. My head was turned the next year by his September,1968, photos of John and Ann Heider's home birth, a revolutionary leap away from the medicalization of women's bodies and rituals. Could it be true that the very natural function of labor and delivery must be confined to a hospital or could it occur outside under a tree? It turned out the tree was illegal. Women wanted it anyway. It would take years to sort these two camps out.

With these credentials, I expected George to throw off his cloak of familiarity and go highbrow on me. I expected him to ignore Paul when they met at the coffee pot in the lodge. I never expected him to go out of his way to set me up with a safe ride back to the city. But he did. He cared about Esalen and he cared about the staff. He was older than the hippie generation, and his genteel southern upbringing and family life precluded the beatnik phase except for an occasional highball at Alan Watt's houseboat. Now he thought we were onto something important, a new impulse in America.

I bought the magazine. I still have it. His eyes opened mine to the surge of the times and acknowledged the significance of my private revolution. This was bigger than me, more than my travel-partner relationship with Paul. This was a ground swell, a richer way of living life more fully, closer to the ground, economically self-sustaining without a lot of stuff, and most significantly, united in opposition to the Vietnam War in a faraway delta, fighting Viet Cong who were maybe just locals. We were living out the mantra "Make love not war". We took It seriously.

Esalen® Massage: Adding Layers

Paul drew the night shift again. After a half hour passed with no action and no shadows moving in the night, he turned to me. "How about I give you a massage at the baths?" A massage? I had never even seen a massage and certainly never considered receiving one. Today's sexual revolution invited women to take back control over their wellbeing and make healthy choices. This particular evening my back ached from carrying my duffle. Why not?

    Paul set up one of the wooden plank tables on the Bathhouse's south side, neatly spreading out two bath towels and locating a plastic bottle of clove-scented oil. I lay down, pleasantly comfortable in the steamy air. He began applying slow strokes down my back. Unsure of the process, I held my breath. "Breathe, baby," he intoned. I exhaled. Something was happening and I felt my control slip away. I wanted to hold on but I couldn't. I felt my body inside, different than a mirror. My shoulders dropped and my buttocks released their habitual hold. "Just relax," he urged, and so I spent the next 20 minutes trying to do something I had rarely considered: just relax. Images played across my consciousness when he rotated my ankle. I recalled yesterday's stumble. The deeper breath I released a moment later cleared out an old asthma memory. I don't give my physical condition much thought; I hated sports; I couldn't touch my toes without bending my knees; yet I was always first on the dance floor because I loved the freedom and the ecstatic high. The slow strokes developed into a percussive rhythm and the tapotement style interrupted my reverie. I felt as if I were under attack by grasshoppers. I raised my head in protest at this changed pace. He caught my signal and pronounced, "Time to turn over." After sleeping on the ground for three months in our hidden encampment, my neck had developed a significant kink and begged for help. His fingers insistently stroked it, from the side, up the back, and soon I could look to left and to right again. What a relief! He smiled, and didn't follow up all this touch with erotic suggestions. What's more, my life at that moment seemed, well, almost calm. Did I mention that he was fully naked, wearing a towel, and I was fully naked wearing nothing? This turned out to be an equalizing factor and I did not feel analyzed or judged. I rolled off the table, took Paul's hands in mine, and smiled back directly into his blue eyes.

This newfound art of sensing and focusing into the body, rather than avoiding it, caught my attention. Bernie Gunther, a physical education teacher from UCLA, studied Charlotte Selver's sensory awareness exercises and popularized her work with his large groups of workshop participants tromping around Esalen's vast front lawns. We easily spotted their slow-paced walk. "Oh, one of Bernie's groups." The participants looked intently at each other and stroked each others' faces; they fed each other orange slices blindfolded. It looked really weird, touching, but not sexual. Then, astonishingly, Bernie led the whole group down to the baths where they disrobed in broad daylight and then briefly stroked each other's bodies with feathery finger strokes. They also poured buckets of cold water on each other. All this stunned and puzzled my revolutionary anti-war mentality, yet it somehow seemed to fit in. These people were educators and clergy and Hollywood folks, with a few well-off college students thrown in. I considered myself really hip, maybe even an intellectual, but this, "Too far out for me," as I described it to Ellen. She snorted, too. Silly! And scary.

Paul had been leader of the Early Morning Mountain Hike at Rancho La Puerta, a healthful retreat center over the Mexican border for rich Beverly Hills denizens and those who wanted to shed a few pounds painlessly while listening to poetry. He led groups off into the desert with jokes and a hearty "Hey, let's go!" attitude. He evoked a sense of ease and fitness. The slow pace and self-conscious stepping he witnessed on the spongy Esalen lawn puzzled him, and he caught Bernie mid-stride at lunch to ask him why not make it easy? Bernie responded that the intent was to "bring awareness to our habitual behavior." Paul, ever the innovator, immediately started trying this on.

"Stop! Ok, what were you doing just now?" he'd bark as I was complaining my way up another mountainous incline. Before long, I began to identify this drudgery thought pattern even before he pounced. Could it be that the real issue was not the incline but the complaining? Over time, I actually came to enjoy the feeling of strong legs beneath me as I hoisted my way upward to the triumphant arrival at the top of each hill.

Esalen's massage staff was small and uncertain. Molly Schackman headed it up and combined her Swedish style with Bernie's sensory experiments. The best part was Storm, the graceful longhaired dancer and artist who fairly floated across the lawn even when she was fully pregnant. When Storm lit a candle, you felt you had just witnessed an ancient ritual. She approached every massage as if entering a prayer or trance and the results could be miraculous. Lars, another massage practitioner, was just the opposite, rambunctious and quick, but fully focused as he plied this new-found art. These two provided most of the massages down at the bathhouse. Although the massages cost less than twenty dollars, they were way beyond my bankroll. Instead of learning from the practitioners' hands, I learned from their lifestyles.

I Wore Flowers In My Hair When I Met the Anti-Hippie Lars

In the Esalen lodge, a handwritten sign hung over an empty basket next to the hot coffee pot: *25¢ cup*. Usually, I reached into my woven shoulder bag and rummaged through it until my fingers felt the coin. Today, I'd forgotten my bag, left hanging from the tree limb back at the campsite. I needed that coffee. It smelled exactly right. I squared my shoulders and poured myself a cup, feeling slightly guilty. Next time I'll pay for it, I promised myself.

I moved out onto the deck to enjoy the steaming brew. I was tired. Staying up with Paul on the night shift wore me down. My steady diet of fig newtons dipped in yogurt wasn't cutting it. I took a sip gratefully, reluctant to join the laughing young women seated nearby, waving me over. I felt unmoored this morning, alone. I wasn't a stoner like them, with their easy laughter and repartee. Neither was I naïve like the wide-eyed students wandering through, displaying their pricy ethnic identity badge of Zuni jewelry to local rip-off artists. I considered myself hip. Was I a hippie? Make love not war resonated. The communal share-all lifestyle didn't. I didn't have a Hindu guru. I did have half a joint in my pocket, saved for Paul.

"Hey!" A terse masculine call interrupted my reverie. Across the deck bounded a slim man in loose pants and no shirt. His spry gait contrasted with his fly-away gray shoulder-length hair and beard. "Did ya pay for that coffee?" he demanded, loudly. He moved quickly, noisily sweeping a table back into place and bumping a bench over to the side. "Damn hippies," he muttered.

"Can't clean up after themselves." He looked up at me, clearly waiting for my response.

I froze like a deer, shamed, head hung, cheeks hot. I quickly lifted my chin and regained my composure. "I'll pay tomorrow. I'm Paul's friend." I explained, putting on my most innocent half-smile, sweeping my hair behind my ears.

"Hmmm," he shook his head. "Where's he camping, I wonder." He looked down, with a thoughtful pause. Maybe he'd noticed our secret site. Again, my alarm bells went off. "I'm Lars," he added. I looked at him more closely and introduced myself. There was something familiar about him.

"I've seen you dance at the Avalon!" I exclaimed. One night last winter I'd taken a low dose of LSD and opened myself to the possibility, the reality, the freedom, of dancing at the Avalon Ballroom. I recalled the man now in front of me, spinning fast through the huge room, strobes flashing. We all moved out of the way when he came through and he seemed not to notice. He was on his own, letting the melody lift his movements, arms flinging away any possibility of a dance partner. The music entwined sitars and drums, then a guitar, joined in, and I too spun away in a different direction. I considered the possibility that I might be a dancer.

Now he stood up, extended his chest, and smiled wide. "Yeah!" he breathed. "I try to get up there at least once a month. Nothing like it. Don't care for all that music especially, just some of it, but, "and here he paused, "I sure do like to dance in that hall, all those pretty girls and I get in for free, too. Somebody noticed my dancing. I took some ballet when I lived in LA but I'm trying to get rid of all that now." Just like that, I was in. By the end of the conversation, he let me know that he was driving up to the city in his VW bug on Saturday after he finished changing the oil. I was welcome to ride along if I wanted.

The following Saturday found me in his VW, sitting on the floor in what would normally be a back seat. His driver's seat was intact and upright. All the other seats had been removed in favor of pillows and a bedroll in the corner. I recovered from my surprise and fluffed up the larger pillows to stack them so I could almost see out the window. I curled my legs up and sat tall. seeing mostly sky and the barren rocky cliffs.

He drove the road easily, seldom using the brake but preferring to down-shift through all the sloping bends and uphill grades. On long downhill runs he pushed in the clutch and coasted, "To save gas." Just as I finally got comfortable, he roused me with an excited, "I'll be damned! Would you look at that!" He stopped the car and jumped out. I did too, expecting a problem. He pointed toward the eastern hills. "They're already out again. California poppies. Didn't expect 'em "til next month." I squinted and the golden hillside came into clear focus. Had it not been for his high-pitched enthusiasm, I would have missed the golden mass of flowers proudly swaying amongst the grasses in the back of an overgrown pasture. He gawked contentedly for a moment. Then, "C'mon, let's go," he gestured, and we moved quickly back into the VW, heading north. I soon realized that he slept in his car on these trips. He dropped me off at my front door on Duboce street without hitting on me or asking to use the bathroom.

Lars lived on the North side of the Esalen property in a one room cabin he'd designed himself out of gathered scrap wood, branches, and driftwood. He added windows salvaged from abandoned cabins and a single sideways French door panel. Its western face cantilevered out over the ocean cliff, so he secured it to a nearby tree with guidewires as insurance. A shovel in the side yard indicated bathroom etiquette. His small cabin lacked most amenities, and its subfloor food box kept just enough veggies for a day or two. His chipped metal sink boasted one working facet: cold. Jars of rice and oatmeal and a can of tomatoes lined one wall, and a dented pan sat atop a propane burner. An oil painting-his?- filled out the corner. The bed was large, tucked into a corner with a comfy foam pad cut to its shape. But the blanket was scratchy wool. Roughhewn, with its many sizes and shapes of windows, the cabin spoke to the innovation that I too was seeking, life without the conventions of 90° angles, an esthetic that flung aside planning in favor of art that simply emerged. All the building supplies were found objects. His only expense was the nails to hold it together.

Last year he'd learned massage from Molly Schackman and now he was half the massage crew, a job he cherished. "My own hours," Lars bragged. He did everything for himself and expected the same of his co-workers, an expectation that always fell short. In his own fashion, he reached out to help me and to help others who came and went. At the same time, his dislike for freeloaders, those who didn't clean or work or drank too much, was often in evidence. He winced at Paul's harangues about flying saucers. He'd never ask anyone for a dime.

Yet he painted in oils, designed every aspect of his patchwork cabin, and possessed a finely-honed sensuality. I called him a lifestyle artist. He had few luxuries and saved his money. He played out his role in this community with a broom and a hammer, always fixing what others had neglected, often scowling, an enforcer of rules that someone like me might be overlooking. His massage was nearly brisk yet very effective. Clearly, he loved the massage work, enjoyed helping a client from LA unload her city drama and come to her senses. He especially liked to massage beautiful women and was the only practitioner who refused to work on anyone over 165 lbs. He himself didn't set much value in relaxing. A good vacation was a monthlong motorcycle ride. He drank an occasional glass of jug wine and didn't smoke weed. Or tobacco.

I soon met up with Lars again, this time in the baths. The hot springs waters were siphoned into a trough with spigots that opened to large square cement baths or white claw-footed tubs. Looking out toward the crashing sea to the west, I slowly lowered myself into the slippery sulfur water, mindful of the heat and hoping it was as beneficial as Paul claimed. I stretched my legs out full length in this large bath, loving the way my body bobbed up to the surface, made extra buoyant by the heavier mineral water. Ah, this was the life! I closed my eyes—and at that very moment a huge splash came out of nowhere, right next to me, rocking my waters. Now my hair was all wet and my peace disturbed. Alarmed, I opened my eyes to see Lars leaning back, head tied tight in a white towel turban, blissfully relaxing. This pause lasted only a moment or two. Then up he rose, again splashing water everywhere. He sprang from the large tub into one of the white claw-footed tubs. His howl let me know it was filled with cold tap water. He wiggled and shook and rolled his now-ruddy body over. Another pause, more loud exhales of pleasure. "Ok, gotta go," he muttered and jumped out. Every time he jumped, his penis jumped, too, and this seemed to delight him. He took his towel and slapped his body every which way until he was semi dry. I thought he was going to pee over the railing down the cliff like little boys do, but he just looked westward and headed for his clothes. He acknowledged my presence with "Now that's a bath!" and a grin. I noticed the short-haired woman in the far tub had re-organized herself so that she didn't have to look.

I struggled to applaud this open display of Lars' body with no hint of modestly covering his groin. No fig leaves here. I swallowed back my judgement and smiled. I stepped out of the bathtub. Standing tall, I stretched into my side body, no longer bound by my formfitting Maidenform bra. I smiled with pleasure at feeling my body without the constraints of undies, socks, and waistbands, feeling my whole length. I skimmed my fingers from my wrist to my thighs. The following week I posed naked in the forest performing t'ai chi poses for a local photo shoot while swatting away a swarm of mosquitoes.

Still, I sensed the subtle disconnect between proudly owning every part of my body without shame and the corresponding titillation of naked women in the popular culture. The prospect of living this fully, this openly, took real strength and commitment on my part. I could dance bare breasted at a community birthday celebration or attend a harvest party in the hills wearing my bikini. Yet a local reporter would call this dirty dancing and equate nudity with sexy in the *San Francisco Chronicle*. One hitched ride included the driver's attempt to pinch my perky breasts, evident through my stretch nylon shirt. Hey! When he asked candidly why I didn't wear a bra, I responded indignantly, "You try wearing one. That tight band around my chest keeps me from breathing." Then I exited the car. As I took a giant step forward to enjoy my body and own it fully, to be respectful, circumspect, yet sometimes naked, I felt these tentacles of mid-century culture grip me, pull me back from the brink, urge me to cross my knees, become defensive, and forgo the urge to express with arms and legs spread wide.

Later I would sign up to receive a series of bodywork sessions. When the practitioner initiated the deep Rolfing realignment on my lower back, my butt tightened reflexively. OK. I breathed into it. Yet despite my best efforts, the old habits held tight and constrained my leg, inhibiting a free swing at the hips. Letting go of my gluteals, my butt, seemed initially impossible. Not only would I be forced to drop my defense of warding off sexual advances, but I also had to go back further to pre-teen modesty and even earlier to bathroom anxiety. Most significantly, my legs were my escape. If I allowed my legs to relax, maybe I wouldn't be able to walk uphill to get home. I'd be weak. Or maybe I wouldn't be able to run if I had to. Flight. I sighed a deep exhalation and let my hip bones release into the massage table's foam padding for just this minute.

Turning me over to the face-up position, my bodyworker slowly stretched my leg across my body for a yummy feeling. When he let my leg swing back, I snapped to attention and held on lest my crotch be exposed. My body, it turned out, would only be as free as my mind allowed.

Many of Esalen's guests sought out the institute because they wanted to spark change in their lives; they wanted something different. Sometimes this was an intellectual pursuit, an idea in need of administration and funding. Some were simply stuck, seeking to identify and release an old story. For others, like me, it was a full-on upending of life as we'd known it. Lars, too, fell into the latter category, especially when it came to living in nature. He used forest and beach found objects as his artistic medium. He was so focused on his surroundings that he gathered a large collection of arrowheads by simply watching where he walked.

One morning I came across Lars bustling down the beach path beside the original Murphy residence known commonly as the Big House. A slightly older stiffer fellow in leather shoes, Bermuda shorts with knee socks, sweater, canvas hat and a walking stick followed him awkwardly. "Ecologist," Lars waved an introduction. In a word he drew the distinction between one who studies nature and one who lives in it. "Wants to go out in my boat." Lars kept a small aluminum rowboat tucked into the cliff beneath the Big House. I'd seem him haul it out and then set its nose into the surf, rowing like crazy until he cleared the breaking waves. I was pretty sure the ecologist's shoes were going to get wet.

Lars wasn't the kind of person I grew close to. Yet I trusted him and grew to accept his scowl and his sudden lighthearted change of mood. He'd come to Esalen in the footsteps of a psychiatrist, Dr. Larry Ranselhoff, who he befriended in LA. He'd kept his sailboat in the shrink's garage. After he experienced Big Sur on a motorcycle trip, he sold the boat and moved north, arriving in 1965. Now he was determined to keep Esalen natural the way he wanted it and to help out any way he could. He always found something else in need of fixing or cleaning. Yet his name is not fated to make it into the Esalen History book.

Lars never joined us on the lawn for an afternoon toke of weed. He watched us from afar. He aligned with Esalen's maintenance designer, Selig Morganrath, and with the other old timers who'd been at Esalen since '63. While they found the young people drifting down from San Francisco's Haight Ashbury amusing and colorful, they didn't extend a welcome mat. Other youth or middle-aged misfits drove up from Laurel Canyon in LA with sharper elbows and they too were entertained and waved out on Sunday afternoon.

In this community at Esalen and the surrounding canyons and ridges, early sojourners had arrived seeking a freer way of living. After the first damp winter in jerry-rigged shacks of foraged wood, they settled on self-reliance, freedom of expression, and friendship with their fellow Bohemians to get them through. They planted chard and watered their gardens. Meanwhile, the free-wheeling hippies sipped on nature without noticing its rhythm of seeds dropping, tiny sprouts, full blown greens for dinner. The hippie work ethic—or lack of it—puzzled these locals who weren't prone to give handouts. Posed as politically radical, most hippies weren't actively political at all. Their love-flavored social life inspired a full-fledged VD epidemic that the *San Francisco Chronicle* gleeful reported.

Eventually Esalen rescinded Lars' rental agreement, if there was such a thing, and Lars moved on. With his frugal lifestyle, he'd saved enough money to purchase a small shack in nearby Palo Colorado Canyon. When he was in his mid 50's, he realized he was lonely and announced he wanted a female partner. His quest took less than a year. I have photos of their wedding. He is in a dark suit; she is in a white dress; all the local drummers are playing. They were truly in love; he actually glows. The frosting on their cake: she turned out to be wealthy.

Full Moon in August

Esalen circa 1967 had a pace all its own. On the one hand, the seminarians, as we called the workshop participants, walked up to Fritz's meeting room to attended scheduled classes, taking copious notes from leaders who would soon become famous. They sat in groups of two, "dyads," and experienced parts of themselves as uncharted as Columbus' ocean, with tears or pounded fists. For the rest of us, we worked, we got stoned on Mexican marijuana at four pm, we headed down for staff hour at the baths at five o'clock. We waited in the evening shadows till the bar keeper turned up the music in the lodge, or better yet, till the drummers arrived. After dark we pushed the tables back and danced. When the music stopped, we exploded out onto the redwood plank deck to sit around the open fire pit, as a few local pickpockets prowled their way through the parking lot.

    Dancing was something I did by myself, dropping into the music and letting it move me, lift my arms and twirl me out the door onto the deck beneath the stars. This wasn't performance art. Sometimes I mimicked my friend Seymour's frenzied high-stepping beat in his red fire eater's shirt, or flung my boyfriend a tossed nod over my shoulder. "You're always dancing away!" Paul exclaimed. Sometimes I caught sight of a lone soul on the sidelines and invited him in. Mostly though, I swayed to the beat and allowed it to wake me up. *"Ride Sally Ride"* got me moving with its horse-like rhythm; *The 'Time Has Come Today*, belted out by the Chambers brothers with its tick-tock rhythm and its eleven-minute slow-down rift, forced me to drop in. *"My soul has been psychedelicized!"* they shout. The music slows, then speeds up int classic rock. A wild electric guitar comes out of right field, hypnotic, human screams, all the while with a relentless beat

Full Moon in August

maintained by the drum. I swoop and turn, mindless, and let the stars spin above me. The moon rises high in the midnight hour.

On this particular night, the place is jammed. Hitch-hikers stroll down the hill and charm the gate guard with their stories. The dishwasher closes up shop early. Locals slip between the Eucalyptus trees and emerge on the dance floor. Gerald, the bartender, has that new album: the Beatles *Sergeant Pepper's Lonely Hearts Club band.* He picks up the phonograph needle and places it on *All You Need Is Love,* with its jazzy breaks and harmonics. In my loose cotton pants and blue leotard, I twirl freely around the floor of the lodge, pass the coffee machine, and feel the space surround me. One by one, others join me, as George and the boys repeat, "Love is all you need." Pretty cool. Then the barkeep turned the volume up and spins the disc again. More people join in, and sparks start to fly between the dancers. Not sexual. Not cutsie. This electricity said something about community, about unity, about how we were all in this together and anything could happen. The sky's the limit. I reached out, touched a nearby woman, a passing man. Our bodies attuned to each other and a hundred people danced together, blowing the roof of the lodge with positive energy. This was IT, I concluded, all you need is love.

After the disc spun a third time, we cheered, tears streamed, and we separated, overwhelmed by the intensity of this connection. I sat by the outdoor fire and let the full moon beam down. When I looked up, I became aware that all the "heavies" were present: Peter Melchior, whose gentle demeaner and drop of Indian blood calmed anyone out of their bad trip; Phil Rogers, a stocky quiet local who intuitively knew when trouble was on the way and arrived before it did. Sure enough, within minutes a tall skinny boy, newly arrived, started yelling with anger at the government. An ex-soldier? Peter stood slowly, looked him in the eye, agreed about the misguided folk back in Washington, and the boy all but fell into his arms. Meanwhile, Phil calmed a shout-down between two late night musicians. Next minute, they picked up their instruments and swung into a matching rhythm.

I felt the tingle in the air and the amped-up energetic swirl, strong enough to attract a car off this lonely road and down Esalen's driveway, a woman out of her husband's arms, or a man who sees unfriendly visions to don his knife, only to slip it back into its sheath. In the hills, the coyotes howled, one den answering another. Death seemed closer here. A simple stumble could land me on a beach two-hundred feet below. I wouldn't be the first. So, I sat by the fire and gazed into the flames, facing tantalizing questions about who I was now and what would become of me in this wild and free place, this jutting plain on the edge between the Santa Lucia Mountains and the sea. The Essalen tribe with their forgotten shell mounds seemed very close to me now. I looked for assurance in the flames and saw only brilliant dancing light.

Through the lodge windows I could see my new pal, Seymour, still dancing, now circled by his latest girlfriend and a bevy of newcomers just learning to wave their arms skyward and use their voices. They raised their knees and leapt one foot to the other on the drum's beat. He wore his faded red embroidered fire-eater shirt and let the music and the crowd move him. I rose to rejoin the dance, not finding any easy answers in the dying flames. Who was this guy, Seymour, who baked, massaged, carried around Fritz's gestalt books, and now magnetically held forth on the dance floor? Maybe he knew something.

The Lion Speaks Tonight: Changing Names

I met Seymour on my second visit to Esalen. I had hitched from Haight Street to join my travel companion lover, Paul, who hugged me upon arrival and then proclaimed, "You have to meet Seymour." I immediately understood that in this outlier's world, Seymour counted. We walked hand in hand downhill on the springy lawn toward a staff group where a dark-bearded man sat combing his fingers softly through his companion's hair as she lay in his lap. She sighed contentedly.

"I like your art!" asserted Seymour immediately when Paul introduced us. He sat up, disengaging his hand. My art. He was referring to my hasty colorful sketches decorating Paul's letters. I didn't know yet that everyone scanned the common mailbox, so my free-form flowers and scribbled street scenes were on full view. He looked directly at me and smiled through his beard. I looked away, feeling a hot flush of embarrassment. I took a breath and lifted my eyes to smile back at his compliment. I wanted to be an artist, but most people didn't notice. He did. "Gotta go to work," his voice lifted, changing the mood entirely. He leaped up and strode off across the spongy grass toward the baker's kitchen. Later I saw him playing chess and laughing with the same girl. He seemed sexy in a safe way, no talk of "I want you forever," or "I must have you now." Just humor and fun and a roll on the lawn. The girl on the lap sat up now and smiled at me welcomingly.

I joined the staff group as Paul's girl. My legs were unsteady in this new setting. Most of the time I didn't say much. In this crowd, immediacy, the here and now, counted for more than the college degree you planned to get. The interior part of me—who wanted to be an unfettered artist, fought for civil rights and marched against the war—stood in a fierce stalemate with the part of me who needed a lover to feel ok, doubted the wisdom of drugs, and needed to have a few dollars and a comb in my pocket. I kept these thoughts to myself.

Yet Seymour had the affront to tease me about being straight, to bust me on a secret romantic tryst, to notice me, look right at me and accept me as I was. I sensed his secrets, too, suspected his jailbird background, admired the part of him that stared shame in the face and told stories about his aluminum siding sales scams and how he arrived on the Esalen staff as a dishwasher to pay off his bar bill. He loved sex, he loved to fall in love again, he liked the edge. He'd worked in carnivals and ate fire on the full moon in August. He danced bare-chested with knees raised high. His beard posed a fire hazard he chose to ignore. He bravadoed over a rotten childhood and two youthful marriages.

His one regret was his lack of schooling. To fill in that hole, he moved in with the big boys, the leaders who demanded full commitment, twenty-four hours a day. He rode with them—Fritz Perls, John Heider, Dick Price, Ida Rolf, Charlotte Selver and Charles Brooks—to emerge a skilled group gestalt leader. His therapeutic stance interwove his existential body-mind skill and art philosophy with his carny North Beach character. He mocked the spiritual trapping of the new age and rejected astrological clichés about his Leo personality. "Do you really believe that stuff?" he asked dismissively. He chose instead to meet each facet of himself, to resource every part, including "the terrorist within." "I've got one." He admitted with a grin, and challenged me to meet my own inner terrorist. Me? Only toward the government, those warmongers.

By example, he taught me to lift my voice in protest when the situation demanded, or to respond honestly to my lover about the depth of my feeling. I stood a little straighter and began to enjoy my own wild dance late at night in the lodge. I dodged my quick call to self-judgment and tempered my resistance at being told what to do. In the ensuing years, I often dialed down my commentary, while he persisted in speaking up from his core at high volume.

Many traditions embrace name change as a symbolic gesture of rebirth or renewal. In its simplest form, a wife joins her husband's family and assumes his name. In a spiritual tradition, undertaking one's studies is often affirmed with the gift of a new Sanskrit name, or joining an order and becoming a brother, as in Brother John. Upon a remarkable recovery from illness, the survivor might assume a new name to serve as a reminder of miracles.

The notion of changing one's name to memorialize a life-changing moment was not lost on Seymour Carter when he abandoned his birth name. This new name allowed him to escape an identity that included broken families and jail time. "See more", he said, laughing, and he meant it. Originally trained in art, he saw gestalt in its root sense as a perceptual skill. In his groups, he held up a black line drawing. Is It two people in dialog, or is it a vase?

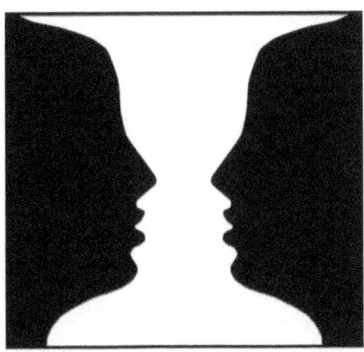

Seymour's brother, Michael Sohns, suggested to me that Seymour took on his new identity when he left Seattle bound for San Francisco, in 1965. "I didn't know him as Seymour until 1967 when I visited Esalen. I'd heard he, Gary, was there, and I found him giving a massage down in the baths. We didn't recognize each other at first." The beard might have been one factor.

"I learned a lot in jail." Seymour recounted one day. "They put me in the library." He did less than a year for his drug charge, but this may have led to his dropping Gary Sohns and emerging fresh as Seymour Carter. No more jail residue, and also no more child support.

Years later, Seymour would take on a third name, *Ojo Pojoque*, meaning *the eye of the casino*, reportedly delivered to him during a vision quest in New Mexico. Seymour felt an affinity with Native Americans and likely had a significant measure of their DNA in his veins. The Ojo Pojoque was the native lookout on the casino floor, watching for scammers. "He spelled it differently each time," smiled his pal, Bill Herr.

Seymour encouraged others to get a fresh start with a new name, too. In 1968 he met Cheryl, who owned an MG but sometimes preferred to hitchhike down from San Francisco. "I'm Cheryl, not Sheryl," she often found herself saying firmly with a smile. A San Francisco debutante and Sarah Lawrence grad, Cheryl landed an Esalen job as a waitress and later as a practitioner on the massage crew down in the steamy hot springs. She watched the sea otters happily loll on the waves and heard them break abalone shells on their chest. She descended the mucky cliff edge from the baths to the beach and gathered handfuls of the iridescent shell shards. She listened for the Indian chanting she "heard" in the evenings in the tubs. She loved Seymour's wild full moon fire dancing and unconventional thinking. They moved in together.

Their new home was one of the vintage wood-paneled house trailers parked near the garden area. It lined up with five other trailers, Esalen's answer to staff housing. While Cheryl focused on nature, Seymour sat in their tiny living room and focused his binoculars on the noonday crowd entering the lodge for lunch. "Now Bobbie's with John!" he chortled.

They plotted a trip to New Mexico to get closer to the Native American spirit and incidentally to trade off the shells. Cheryl had seen abalone fragments worked into Navaho silver jewelry, so she suspected they might be a valued commodity. "We're hitching to Taos," she announced to me one afternoon." They set off with backpacks, a pouch of seashells, and sleeping bags. At night, they slept in the bushes by the side of the highway. It was easy to get rides, especially since Seymour would stand back and she would be the one stretching out her thumb and tossing her long curly hair in the wind.

Credit: Paul Herbert

The second or third day out, a carload of ex-cons picked them up. They fell into talking about jail days. Seymour jumped right into the discussion about their jail names. Cheryl noticed that even under these circumstances, she felt completely safe. "Seymour had been in jail. I trusted; I was with a guy who had been there, done that. I felt completely safe. I was," she added, laughing, "kind of dumb, but it worked."

As she listened, the concept of changing her name appealed to Cheryl. "I had always hated my name. Everyone mispronounced it. What a perfect opportunity. I will change my name too. The name *Samantha* came into my mind." She declared her new name and "Seymour loved it."

The pair journeyed on to Taos, feeling safe and free on the highway. Once there, they located the town square where all the Navajos sat, silent, with their wares. They walked up to an elder round woman with her native blanket, selling jewelry. Samantha knelt and greeted her respectfully, then untied her bundle. "She was very happy to see all that abalone." Samantha pointed to a heavy turquoise necklace among the woman's wares, strung with large platelets of deep blue turquoise like a coil, finished off with a few coral beads. "I'll trade for this." The grey-haired Navajo woman agreed without bartering.

Samantha put the necklace on immediately and wore it daily, a talisman of her new identity. Her decision to let go of her given name, Cheryl, was based on more than just a pronunciation problem. She wanted to leave behind her sheltered, conservative

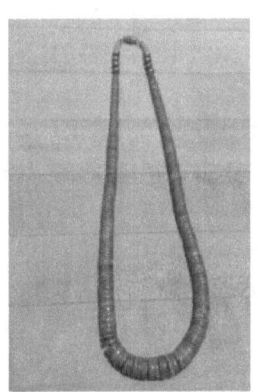

upbringing. "By high school, I'd never even met anyone who lived in an apartment. I was happy to leave behind the old name with all its trappings and start fresh as a Big Sur hippie momma, no bra or underpants. When I came back to Esalen, I told everyone to call me Samantha and no one even remembered that I had another name."

She shared her new identify the first day they returned; Today, only her accountant and her family know her as Cheryl. She continued to strive for the fresh new identity in alignment with the seasons, as described in her recent poem.

Autumn
Cozy enveloping warmth turns to fresh wind, I wonder at the miracle of change.
Perhaps I could loosen my summer arms,
releasing enveloping embraces, forgo fragrant kisses,
welcome the discriminating glance,
present you with my Autumn mood.

As for Seymour, he was constantly tinkering with his nomenclature.

"Seamy", he said sometimes, with a punk smile. Usually, he preferred the professorial Seymour image with the black-rimmed glasses that we see in this photo with John and Anne Heider and Dick Price. He embraced gestalt practice's awareness of multiple selves, and tried on most characters he came in touch with. Besides the carnival performer, he saw himself as anthropologist, health practitioner, psychologist, criminal, skier, hiker, native artist. Thankfully, he gave up auto racer. We don't know what he was gifted to see—he certainly shied away from images of seer or psychic, although he did seem to have some of those abilities—and he was consistent in his quest for rebirth and freshness. He chose to see things as they are: plain, simple and filled with vitality. When it came to confrontation, he was one of the best. Authority had no dominion over him. Yet he never gained in-group status. Later he scrawled the following in his notebook: *Who am I?*

WHO AM I?
I AM ESALEN'S RESIDENT ALIEN, A SECULAR SKEPTIC IN A UTOPIAN COMMUNITY.

I AM A DEVOTEE OF SURREALISM, IRONY, AND THE FRACTURED NATURE OF IDENTITY

I AM A MAVERICK SOCIAL SCIENTIST, THE SURVIVING MEMBER OF ESALEN'S TEAM OF THERAPISTS WHO REVOLUTIONIZED PSYCHOTHERAPY IN THE 1960s.

Dropping Out

No doubt about it, I was trying to lose my mind in this utopian community. Bernie Gunther would title his photo book, *Sense Relaxation Below Your Mind,* with a back cover directive, "Get out of your minds and back in your body."

"Dumb," I proclaimed when I first saw it. Too hip. Yet I made it my personal off limits to think too much about what I was doing, where I was going.

Another mantra, this one from Aldous Huxley's Island, rose up to meet me, *"Be here now."* How could I ruminate, worry about leaving my marriage, no career path, partaking in psychedelic drugs? I couldn't. I'd be buying into the norm, the expectations of the rising middle class aligned with the military complex and racism. I developed a mental strategy to just do something else when a doubtful thought rose. Wasn't I truly living what those shrinks and professors were philosophizing about? Paul and I dropped out with no car, no spare change, just our camaraderie and our belief that the pathway to our natural authentic selves lay ahead once we managed to drop our inhibitions.

Yes, I entertained aspirations. I wanted to save the world by getting to the roots of aggression. I wanted to make land more accessible. I wanted more music. A good man who adored me. All good aspirations. All too big to manifest.

I had attended the epoch-defining 1967 Be-in in Golden Gate Park where once again Richard Alpert opened my eyes. He extolled the thousands of stoned hippies, Hells Angels, and curious neighbors resting on the grass in front of him to "Tune in, turn on, and drop out. And then do it again." In this way, he one-upped his psychedelic colleague, Timothy Leary, who left the future dangling with his "drop out". I heard Alpert; he was speaking to me. "Yes," I said. So did the unshaven guy on my left and the patchouli-scented woman on my right. Pot smoke infused the air.

I heard him, and I felt recognized. Now six months later, I had really dropped out, with no reliable paying gig in my future. My hitch down Route One to Esalen Institute demonstrated this mission. My newly acquired Big Sur community supported me in this ethic. The Esalen dishwasher was an MD. A formerly successful call girl staffed the front desk. Heck, the gate guard was the writer Hunter S. Thompson. "We don't want your stinkin' money," said it all. I was breaking with my tidy, polite upbringing. I argued politics at the dinner table now. I horrified my mother by throwing out the pots and pans I didn't use. My clothes were loose and free with no undergarments to bind my chest.

Still, I didn't know how to survive in this lifestyle. I needed money to buy cheese and brown rice and fig newtons. So, I traveled back to San Francisco and did stint work: I edited and typed; I sewed custom shirts from a pattern I designed; I mostly relied on the Esalen free box of discarded and forgotten items, coupled with luck, to get by. I had no interest in mass production but insisted that each shirt I made be tailored to its wearer. I carefully embroidered around the collar and neck packet of a green cotton pullover designed to disappear in the forest colors. I tie dyed skirts—yellow first, then blue, then a re-dye in yellow to turn some of the blue into green. Spontaneous art, clothes designed at home. I didn't want to abandon my life to go to work.

At Esalen I found my models, the dancers and artists Storm and Marian, who came to Esalen for full moon celebrations. Marian's straight blonde hair was always in motion as she smiled; her twenty-eight-year-old face glowing. She is the one in front in the painting that follows. A well-born Brit, she arrived with an art degree in sculpture. Storm, born Thea, was darker in every way, beautiful, fiery. She was the well-off daughter of a Greek New England family and nearly graduated from a Boston university. She occasionally started the evening with a few words about gathering the wind. Both lived the very life I aspired to, residing in the hills, eating off the land, helping their man tack a cabin together with discarded wood and two-penny nails. They sold their artisan crafts of knots and woven wool at the nearby Nepenthe gift shop. When they walked by, I understood the meaning of grace, the significance of dropping out of mid-century America into a life dedicated to beauty and authenticity. In comparison I lived life on the surface, with head trip convictions but no real action. . .

I had learned to condemn the military industrial complex when I marched against the Vietnam War. I learned that my hoped-for career in journalism was down the tubes because newspapers lie. I hadn't learned how to survive these decisions. These women gave me both hope and a model. They were actually living their values and it worked.

I ate dinner with Marian one night at Esalen. She forked her salad quietly as her partner, Bob Burton, known to us as the Wizard because of his oversized beard, held forth on the Akashic records, the Dead Sea Scrolls, and other mysterious sources of knowledge known only to the initiated. He seemed smart. Not stoned. Marian looked on, nodding in assent. "A big quake comes and Point 16 (their current camp site) will fall into the ocean," he proclaimed. "We're moving." And they did, to a Big Sur homestead further South known as Dempsey flats, a 30-minute drive up a dirt road along the ridge top before dropping down an even more rutted route fronting the Santa Lucia range. They didn't come out often. They had each other, and the goats.

On this summer evening, Marian and Storm joined with drummers Jeffrey Stewart and Storm's unshorn partner Ron Accioli, in the Esalen Lodge for a jam. A piano was unloaded off an old truck and tucked into the corner, and an upright string bass stood ready. The drummers joked amongst themselves, anointed their hide drumheads with fragrant cocoa butter, and began to pound out a rat-tat-tat-tat rhythm. Storm, in airy cottons, and Marian, always in velvety blues and greens, emerged from the back, circled, beckoned us to join in, and taunted the drummers to respond. The beat picked up. Colors swirled, the candles flickered and soon fifty people swayed and sweated on the dance floor, sourcing a more primitive and wilder part of themselves.

I could not sit still. I had to rise, pound my bare feet on the throbbing wooden dance floor, let my short dress swing free as I spun outside, under the stars, ecstatic for a moment. Dropped out? Dropped in was more like it. We pulsated together, apart, building momentum and unlocking forgotten rhythms. I heard the ocean surf whisper between the beats. A woman whooped. I stopped only when a sliver from the redwood deck slammed into my toe. Ouch! I limped to the side and extracted it slowly. I paused to catch my breath.

While we danced, a crowd gathered, watching. "Hey, you really dance great," a paunchy man in his 50s exclaimed to me. I smiled. I looked away. I knew the truth about him. He still worked for the establishment, some sort of a gig in real estate. C'mon! That's still part of the government conspiracy of ownership. I moved away. He wasn't real, wasn't willing to drop out and to let it all go, to rid America from this warmonger society. Neither was the young student guest, eagerly sampling the sex, drugs, and rock culture around him, using his Dad's money to pay his way. A nearby psychologist swayed to and fro, intent on capturing the vibe so he could export it to South Bend, Indiana, as if he'd authored it.

Nope. "I'm committed, fully in," I told myself as I tugged at my loose dress and adjusted the flower behind my left ear. So was

Paul. Our new tribe who gathered for dinner around the open fire under the bridge stood fierce about leaving every aspect of the straight world security behind them. This was our hearth. The sky opened over our heads; no power lines or ceiling got in our way. We dropped out, dropped into a community, eschewing the cowardly weekend warriors who ogled us and then drove home to their "boxes made of ticky tacky" condos. We danced to rid ourselves of those inhibitions that limited our lives. We believed Martha Graham, who taught that each of us had our own unique dance and it was our job to dance it. Serious stuff. We chose to dive deep, or as Paul said, "Far in," experience ourselves, get down and intimate, without stepping back.

"Macramé," explained Storm during a craft guild get-together, "Is a more intimate form of weaving." With deliberate fingers she tied a dozen threads together to create a one-of-a-kind hanging planter case. This cry for connection and authenticity permeated my day and gave cred to my campsite existence with no material comforts and heaps of esthetics instead. As I crawled out of the bedroll at dawn to hang over the hill's edge for my morning pee, I could not imagine living in a room with four walls. Yet sometimes I shivered.

Over time, I learned these magical women had their feet on the ground. Life was not as bucolic as I imagined. Children were born and friends died. Poverty wracked its toll. One woman thrives and one woman is locked in depression. A partner runs off with another woman and then returns on the eve of his new wedding day. A woman finagles a public project and hires her husband to lead it in a desperate attempt to make ends meet. She forgot for a moment about his drug addiction.

These women and these men journeyed to Big Sur as artists, pre-dating Esalen. At one point fourteen people lived in the lofted Esalen Art Barn. They lived as artists live everywhere, skirting poverty, well-acquainted with feast or famine. Peter Melchior, a local poet, musician and Esalen manager explained to me, "At the beginning it was a toss-up; would Esalen go toward art or toward psychology... We started the guild of hands to share artists' work."

He went on to self-publish his poetry; and maintained a small enameling studio in the back room of his home.

His neighbors on the North side of Hot Springs Creek all put in serious studio time. His pal Carl Lee set up a kiln outside the art barn and supplied the lodge with large ceramic bowls, glazed in semi-gloss earth tones. Across the way, Gopher added a studio to his hand-hewn home and fell in love with gemstones. He learned to shape gold into intricate settings and turn opals and amethysts into sought-after rings. Carl switched from those giant salad bowls to intricate jewelry, keeping his designs simple. A classic guitarist, Ger Agee, also known as Gerald Thatcher, tended the bar and edited the catalog.

I bartered for a painting by the artist John Horler, another art barn denizen, before he began his batik phase. Of course, I had the tarot deck John designed and produced, using local characters as models for the various arcane types. His tarot readings were uncannily psychic. I didn't want him to read my cards. Maybe I was afraid of what they would tell--or of the questions I might ask about the future.

John loved a good glass of port wine. He enjoyed several each evening. He slept in the kitchen storeroom, a prized single room. In the morning it was the breakfast waitress' task to awaken him when she picked up supplies for the morning meal. He slept nude. I would learn that waking him up meant that not only was I subjected to his extraordinary surly morning temper, but I was also privy to his waking erection as he stomped from bed and flung the door open. I would beg my kitchen co-waitress to come with me. He was alternately depressed, rageful, drunk, or ecstatically working on the last dye job for his *Swallows Flying* batik designed as a stage backdrop for the Folk Festival.

John could swing wide, from one realm of consciousness to another in an easy arc. He was at home with those seeing visions; he wasn't put off by a screamer in the night. After a talk at Esalen, Allan Ginsberg spoke on behalf of the audience, "We are all in conspiracy together to manifest the experiences that we have had as being more real than that which is taken to be sanity by the official sane makers." (Poetry and Madness at Esalen, 1968). Sanity was under attack and we all applauded. This also meant I sometimes hid in the bushes to avoid a friend's rage or lengthy diatribe, or endured a ride home with a drunk at the wheel asking angrily what did I know about living on the edge? "I'll show you life on the edge...." he shouted as we hurled forward. I learned to pray when prayer was the only hope.

Explosive expression - punching a boyfriend as a heartfelt expression of jealousy, yelling, public tears – received applause and review by the community. The art barn apprentice smashed all his pots. The chef picked up and dumped his large pot of black bean soup in one easy motion five minutes before lunch when a passerby commented off-handedly that it looked like shit. A jealous woman punched a man in the parking lot. It wasn't just staff acting out. One group leader encouraged every group he led to holler "no!" at the top of their lungs. After a week of this, we sat on the lawn and shouted back, "yes!"

Dick Price, co-founder, preferred arm wrestling and would challenge the local drummer when conflict was in the offing. They'd both sit down, one elbow on the table, line up palm against palm and push intently until one hand was finally forced to the table, humiliating the loser. Will Schutz encouraged class members to physically hammer their way through a circle of tightly clasped hands to gain group membership. I scoffed at this and wouldn't do it. Was it the aggression or was it the commitment aspect that put me off?

I was already expert at passive aggression, and I delivered every sarcastic put-down with a flick of my head and one raised eyebrow. Miss cool. Yet, when Paul told me it was time for him to go to Hollywood, get an acting gig, I hollered "No!" He heard me and stayed on this grassy ledge. For a while.

Eavesdropping

The public payphone provided a major source of staff entertainment. Esalen Institute originated as a roadhouse stopover, and the only pay phone at this remote site was conveniently mounted on the redwood wall just outside the main dining lodge. The area was bordered with oversized redwood plank benches that served as our natural gathering spot. We spilled onto the adjacent strip of lawn. On this day I straightened my thigh-length dress and tossed my sandals off. The sun overhead invited us to stretch out. Paul dropped to the lawn and carefully placed his broad-brimmed hat over his face. A co-worker leaned back on his elbows, straining his India print shirt, legs outstretched.

From each of these lounging postures, we could eavesdrop unobtrusively on every word of phone conversation. At this time, Fritz Perls' workshop participants were working intensely on getting past his bullshit radar. "And you will tell him?" Perls inquired after a confessional session. He took a puff on his cigarette. This meant that one attractive 39-year-old woman finally was forced to dial up her long-time LA boyfriend and come clean. We listened in.

She inserted her coins. She knew the number by heart. "Don't come visit, Johnny" She took a breath. "I'm seeing someone here." (Pause). "Yes. Yeah, we're sleeping together." (longer pause and loud sounds through the ear piece.) "Ok, I'll move it." No more coins to insert. Her face was grave, and she wiped her eyes when she fit the phone back in its hanger. She looked over at us. "This isn't easy," she muttered. She rearranged her face into a composed smile, lifting her chin and slipping on dark sunglasses as she strode back to her workshop.

The most touching were the family calls, like this young man who'd been waiting in line to make his collect call. "Hi Dad. Yeah.

(excited) Yeah. I know, I tried to call earlier, but. Anyway, I'm out in California. (pause) Yeah, I know. I'm sorry too. I didn't mean what I said. I'm sorry." (longer pause while he dabs his face with his shirtsleeves). "Ok, good. Susie? We broke up. Yeah. Say hi to Grandma, Give her a hug from me for her birthday. (pause). Uhm, I'm here for a while longer and the van's broken down. Could you send me a check to tide me over? I think they're going to hire me in the kitchen soon. (pause) I know, damn it! I know I just graduated from university, but you just can't imagine how far-out this place is. I want to stay a while. (pause) Yeah, got it, I'll do it soon. Ok, here's my address…."

Then there were the sneak calls made late in the evening placed by the star male group leader. He called his girlfriend every evening. "I really miss you. You're hot. (heavy intake breath). I'm spending my spare time reading, taking quiet walks…group's going great, they love me…gotta go now." The phone clicked off. He didn't notice us on the edge of the lawn. He strode back into the lodge where his lipsticked wife sipped her tea.

Paul and I looked at each other. He shrugged his shoulders with a half-smile. In the midst of my holier-than-thou judgement, I accidentally let myself recall that I too was skipping out on a marriage. At least my husband knew where I was and who had led me here. But he still cared. I didn't want to think about it. I never called him. Certainly not on this phone.

Exiled again in Big Sur

We needed a minute of private time. Paul fixed his focus on his co-worker's brown dusty van in the Esalen parking lot and swung the unlocked door open. Finding it empty, we stepped inside. "Hey," he smiled promisingly, waving a freshly rolled joint of some cheap Mexican stuff. I couldn't quite smile; something felt off. The vehicle's owner, Bill Georgio, had turned himself in yesterday, on a murder charge involving his ex's lover. And here we were, Paul and me, sitting in his abandoned van in the Esalen parking lot. If Paul had pot, he wanted it now, no matter what the circumstance. So, he lit up and the next minute the manager, Bud Leighton, knocked on the window—tap, tap—and busted us.

"You can't be here!" he exploded. I'd forgotten that he was also a lawyer. He knew about evidence, and the ashes we were dropping at that minute might serve as evidence against Bill. "Get out!" he barked sharply. I stumbled over my own feet as I jumped out the rear car door. I knew better. Sometimes with Paul I forgot to think. What followed was an even clearer lesson. "You're 86ed," he added. After hanging out these last six weeks, I knew what that meant. We had to move on. Fired. We skedaddled to our hidden site, packed up our freshly laundered clothes still dangling from the underbrush, and stuffed our other belongings into one bag each. We'd sleep here tonight and depart early. We didn't say much.

Unexpectedly as I departed the next morning, the same boss, Bud Leighton, caught me at the gate and offered me a typing gig. I turned up a few minutes later at the appointed place. The steno machine didn't work, the typewriter was dirty, the rodent-smelling office was in the hallway. I recalled with a rush that office work detail was what I was leaving. I said no thanks and followed Paul up the hill onto Route One.

Paul grinned at me as he tightened my loose bedroll and zipped my overstuffed army surplus duffle. "All set, Babe," He held me to his high standards for road gear. He mocked hitchhiking travelers who sat down on their suitcase and looked wasted, or didn't bother to roll their blankets neatly. Now we stood tall in the wind, thumbs out, headed someplace else. He carried very little, although he now owned a change of dungarees. He remembered to pick up his new gray felt cowboy hat from the gate shack and he wore it now, along with treaded boots. Looking at him in profile I could see the actor, riding Western style in *Bonanza* across our TVs. He looked like James Stewart. "Adios!" he saluted, looking down at the Institute.

Our first ride stopped at Nepenthe. We jumped out with our gear and looked at each other. Nepenthe served as the local Big Sur watering hole. The name in Greek means the last sip of forgetfulness. We counted on that memory haze now in our quest for a hidden campsite. "Let's check out the canyon," he said quietly in my ear.

We walked a short distance uphill on Route One until the shoulder widened on a slow bend in the road. We climbed over the corroded metal highway fence and dropped down the low embankment into a dense redwood forest. The harsh dry hills gave way here to moist air, soft green ferns, fallen trees, and towering coastal redwoods shutting out the sky, their roots seeking the nearby creek water. We slid back to an earlier dream time.

Paul jumped from log to log and I remembered that I needed to replace these leather handmade slick-soled sandals I'd purchased at the Eighth street leather shop in Manhattan. They were made for city pavement, not this vast uneven lifestyle. We stomped in the pine needle duff to check the sloping terrain. A few rays of sunshine slanted through the redwood boughs above. Paul located a level spot near the small, rock-lined creek. Soft! He lay out fallen boughs to border and hide our new camp and within minutes we had a flat new home. The woodsy aromas tingled my nostrils, causing me to wrinkle my nose. Paul wrinkled his in response. Together, we entered an even more secret living situation, outright trespassing in this ancient canyon. The transitions over the fence from highway to canyon could make or break us.

The following day, I hiked out for groceries, a 15-minute hitch away. Now I stood on the shoulder of the road, readying myself for the stumble downward with my duffel shopping bag. Even if I slipped, it wouldn't be bad, just twenty feet of dirt and stones until I reached the comforting cover of the redwood forest. I looked north and south. I listened. The road sounded empty of cars. I heard only the wind, high in the trees. This canyon was our cathedral bedroom, overarched with green boughs and anchored with a two-hundred year old giant log separating our bed from our kitchen eating area. The only problem was the *No Trespassing* sign nailed on the fence and the knowledge that modern-day caballeros stood ready to shoot intruders. It wasn't just a rumor, one of my hitch-hiking friends had already heard gunshots whizzing by. I sighed. I knew land ownership was just one of those myths we had to put up with until things changed.

I tossed down my tan duffle filled with groceries and listened again. Quiet. No sound from Paul. His silence added to my confidence. He'd let me know with a bird whistle if something wasn't right. I stepped off the roadbed, losing my footing and causing a small rockslide. Noisy! I moved fast into the shadows, ducking low over the fence, dodging the moss-covered log, and stepping around the bank of tree boughs we had tossed down to hide any trace of trail. I looked behind me, listened. I heard only the last song of a blue jay in the evening.

Under cover now, I moved freely downhill another hundred feet. "Hey baby!" Paul called from my right. I moved toward the sound, anxious for his presence. I could see his bearded silhouette, never still, singing a quiet song as his cleared our space. He'd already taken off his cowboy hat. He'd artfully arranged a few branches in an old hollow stump into a skeletal peace sign edged with wands of green moss. Now he sat down on a log, lanky legs stretched straight out. He retrieved the crackers from our hidden tin. I pulled the newly purchased cheese out of my duffle. He reached for the water jug, splashing the sweet Big Sur water he'd just collected in the nearby stream. I drank up. "Hey, did you hear the one about the farmer? He went out into his barn one morning and his horse said...." His eyes crinkled up as he guffawed at his own joke. The creek made such a racket we didn't need to be quiet here. A minute later he lit up a thin joint and passed it to me to share. I breathed deep and exhaled just as fully, letting go of my tightly held shoulders, my brace against the world. Overhead, we saw one or two stars appear through the conifer spires. It was time to turn on our lights. I lit the stubby wax candle mounted in a pool of melted wax in a glass jar, a jerry lamp. To my twenty-two-year-old eyes it threw enough light to finish setting up our bedroom.

I pulled out our tightly wrapped sleeping cocoon from under a nearby bough and spread it directly on the slippery-soft redwood needle carpet while he took a splash of the water jug to brush his teeth. My rolled-up jacket would pillow my head. A twig snapped off to our right and we both jolted alert, silent, at attention. A moment passed. Nope, just a branch, maybe the trees growing. We lay down and let the canyon with its crackly sounds and moist pungent scents welcome the darkness in to seal our secret place. We lived here for nearly a month. It turned out we were good at secrets.

We ate our stash of nuts and raisins and peanut butter and bought a few apples from Ed the Mailman's truck when he stopped at Nepenthe. His warm hug and food sales out the back of his truck kept those of us along Route One from starving. Now I purchased only fig newtons and yogurt. In this woodsy area a campfire was out of the question. Next day on our way out, a young man in a heavy flannel shirt appeared almost next to us, going uphill. He looked our way, nodded and kept moving. We knew that he now knew about our campsite. He must be the caretaker. Would he kick us out or steal our stuff?

We stuck out our thumbs and hitched to Carmel for supplies and adventure, purchasing more crackers, luncheon meat, fruit, carrots, and cheese. We shared a plate of egg foo young with tender sprouts and drank pots of jasmine tea at the Chinese restaurant on Ocean Avenue before heading back. I'd never noticed how quickly the days shorten, bumping us into autumn. The Sycamore trees lining the Big Sur valley were already golden. It was time to move on. This canyon was damp and chilly and September was at our back. I shivered and searched for another sweater. We shook the new-fallen redwood needles off our sleeping gear as we settled in for the night.

It's easy to go downhill in Big Sur. My hair hadn't really been clean in a while and I wore the same old colored jeans and clingy tee shirt for a week. I counted my dollars daily. But in today's story, downhill meant following the lay of the land, traipsing the descending canyon pathway, a path into sunlight. "C'mon, honey, It's easy, I've already checked this trail out." Paul coaxed me into crossing a narrow log to get to the North side of the creek.

"You first!" I demanded, holding back. So, to cinch the deal he danced over the log, play-acting falling as he crossed the watery chasm. I took my sandals off and inched my way carefully, taking deep breaths, not looking at the rocks in the rushing creek bed below until I landed on solid land. The path lay ahead through the chaparral and before long we arrived at a broader dirt landing. Looking seaward, I gasped, wide-eyed. I looked at Paul. Whoa! Below us raced the final descent of the Santa Lucia Mountains into the Pacific. A trail zigzagged across the hillside's face. I could see the widest ocean I'd ever seen just a vertical drop away.

I halted and let my breath catch up with me. Paul loped off, almost at a run. He wanted to see where this slope led him, what lay beyond. I could see him grow smaller as he descended. More than anything else I wanted not to fall. I walked on, carefully. After ten minutes of downward drop, switchback after switchback, I'd had it. I sat down on the rocky ground, sweaty. I'd reached my limit. I'd also reached the limit of the continent. Paul sprinted back up the hill to retrieve me. "C'mon baby, you can do it." His smile crinkled his face and that got me. OK. I picked my way down the last hundred feet of loose dirt trail bed, skidding my way downward and scattering a shower of pebbles, close to my possible death. The trail ended abruptly. From here down to the beach was a straight 20-foot drop. No way was I going to do this. A frayed rope lay ten feet down, next to the drop.

Paul sat with me and sang a sea chanty, the one about a drunken sailor. Then he did just what I hoped he wouldn't. He wedged his foot against the highest rock and then scuttled sideways to catch another outcropping with the second foot. From there, he grabbed a sagebrush branch, no real support at all, I could tell. He stood up, turned, and ran, yelling triumphantly the rest of the way down. "It's easy," he hollered up.

My heart beat fast and I considered my options. I could die here. Or, I could drop down to this pristine unexplored beach and join this sandy haired adventurer. He offered up a hand. I wedged my foot against a rock and the pebbles rained down on him. "Hey!" He yelled. I moved more slowly onto a second rock. I slide a bit in these damn sandals and caught the supporting limb of a leaning scrub tree, with a bit of a broken rope hanging off it. Holding firm, I inched the rest of the way, finally letting go to drop the last foot into his arms.

After the cool forest, we were now bathed in sunlight. We locked eyes, silently nodding at our good fortune, and stripping off our clothes. I ran down the beach, arms outspread, loving the space and proud of myself: I had conquered this cliff. The salty Pacific washed my body clean. I had no idea where I was except it felt even more remote than the canyon. I discovered a little nook in the rocks just south, where a stream gently fell over boulders to arrive at its oceanic destination. These toppled rocks were too big to make a comfortable base for our bed rolls. Fortuitously, large timbers lay strewn along the high tide line. I started dragging them and Paul caught on. Our sleeping platform was quickly assembled from someone else's shipwreck.

Walking up hill has always been easier for me. I wasn't so worried about tumbling down. We walked all the way back up the trail along the hill's edge, fording the creek from North to South. I dodged as many poison oak bushes as I could. We picked up our stuff from its hidden cache. I carried my duffle and bag while Paul hauled our blanket roll. We tucked the bananas and cheese into our gear. Going back down seemed much shorter now that we knew our new home by the rushing creek waters awaited us. I managed crossing the log bridge by slipping off my sandals and not looking down ever. I gratefully dropped my duffle by the trail after Paul offered to make an extra trip back to retrieve it.

That night we lay wide awake on our driftwood perch. It would take practice for me to adjust to the symphony of rushing water falling a few feet above our heads and the bass note ocean waves echoing around us. The night sky was bright with more stars than I'd ever seen before. The Milky Way spanned the heavens almost as if to invite us to skip on up. I didn't worry about wild animals yet. I was just learning about Big Sur's wild side.

Something woke me up early. Why not get up? We had no schedule. I wrapped my shirt around me and strolled toward the beach in the half-light of dawn. Barefoot, I started walking toward the shoreline, then stopped dead in my tracks. Was I imagining it, or did something tickle my feet? All around me the wet sand was alive, crawling. Crawling! I rubbed my eyes to make sure they weren't fooling me. Tiny shrimp crawled on the sand along the entire stretch of beach, a quarter mile long. Had they been here all this time? We'd walked on them, danced on them? The layers of ecology snapped into place. Somehow, on this September night, a huge shrimp migration was underway before my very eyes, even though I'd never heard of shrimp in Monterey Bay. I smiled and shook my head in amazement. An hour later they were gone, leaving no trace.

WE HIKE CASTRO RANCH AND DON'T GET SHOT

While heating the morning coffee water over a smoky campfire, I squinted curiously up the waterfall to the stream above it. A small grove of leafy trees interrupted my view of the upper creek-bed. Bent on exploring, Paul scampered up the boulders to the first ledge at the base of the five-foot waterfall. The misty spray caught in his hair and the back of his shirt, making it stick to his body. I could see he was growing muscles every day. He jumped back down to enjoy a peanut butter sandwich with the fresh coffee. "Ahhh." he stretched out for a minute in the sun. Then he glanced at me. "Let's hike out up this canyon for a change," indicating the uphill route above the waterfall.

"Ok, you saw a trail?" I asked.

"Nope." He jumped up and jabbed his shoe into a potential toe hole on the boulder and sprang upward. I tried to follow, but rock climbing is not my skill. I firmed my thighs and gave it a good try. Using the same toe hole, and pushing with my legs and my knees, I managed to reach the first level, a catch-pool above the falls. We continued to ascend and soon the creek swung off toward the North. We stayed with it for a while and then high-tailed it straight up the canyon, leaving the stream. Big Sur taught me that water charts its own course and changes its route often. We were following the creek's earlier bed. This improvised route, without the aid of switchbacks, grew steeper, harder to hike. Sweat dampened my shirt collar. I grabbed at a branch that gave way, skinning my hand. I banged my knee on a rock. "This is too much for me," I complained, in high-pitched exasperation. "Let's go back," I pleaded. Paul carried on. Fifteen minutes later I grew convinced he was trying to kill me. I ran through all the possible reasons. Probably because he didn't like me. By the time we could see Nepenthe to our North, I hated him.

We'd arrived on the North end of the Castro ranch. Local lore said the caretaker was armed and took his job seriously. I transferred my anger at Paul into anger at the caretaker. He imagined he could keep us constrained when clearly the earth had no boundaries. Look at these fences! They were inconsequential in the scheme of things, I concluded. Private ownership has no place in nature. What right have they to fence the landscape in! I begged Paul for a break and we sank into the dry grass, nearly invisible. My legs shook, unused to such a climb.

After a moment's rest, we hiked across a five-acres-wide grassy field, cleared by a century of cattle grazing. Every hair on my body alerted when I spotted a faraway man, my nightmare come true. He raged at us and waved his shotgun. At least it looked like a shotgun at this distance. They hated us hippies here, with our crazy ideas, thinking we can live free on the land. I broke into a fast run and embraced the grimy Route One road post when I finally reached it. From this vantage point, our zig zag switchback trail would be a piece of cake.

A Local Volcano: Grandpa Deetjen

On our return, I found seven folded dollars and a jug bottle of Berbera wine tucked neatly into the driftwood food locker at our beachside camp. An unknown traveler had exchanged the bills for handfuls of our nuts and raisin trail mix. Found money!

Thanks to this windfall, a day later Paul and I were sitting in the Big Sur Inn, enjoying steaming cups of coffee brewed in their old-style vacuum brewer pots. We clanked cups together, toasting "the world's greatest java." The rich fragrance permeated the small unpainted dining room. To add to our pleasure, we shared a generous slice of French Apple pie. That's the one with all the crumbs of sugar and butter on the top crust, with extra cinnamon, made from fresh apples. Deetjens was known on the coast for its baked products, its coffee, and the tall stack of pancakes. The baker came in at four am to make pies, occasional breads, and other delicious baked goods. After our beach cuisine of rice and canned tuna, seaweed, and an occasional vegetable, this fare was our heaven.

Completely sated, I took a good look around the room. Deetjens is a Big Sur historic landmark. built about 1934 as a small end-of-the road inn. Its builder, Helmut Deetjen, emigrated from Norway, perhaps because he wanted to leave home and perhaps because the bridge he built collapsed. Like every old timer in Big Sur, his personal tale was convoluted and shifting, depending on who you talked to. In any case, he built himself a roadhouse, part restaurant with a bar counter between the dining area and the kitchen, and part hotel, with 10 cabins lining the driveway. Castro Creek cascaded through the property on its way to the nearby Pacific. The steep Santa Lucia hillside rose abruptly behind these few

A Local Volcano: Grandpa Deetjen

structures, spitting out little dirt slides even on this autumn day. The construction style, to put it bluntly, was barnlike. The building exteriors were natural redwood, bleached pale over the years. The doors didn't quite fit and gusts of wind blew through the door jam. We'd seen his wife, a granny-looking stout woman, only from afar. She was always on her way somewhere, with a shovel or a broom in hand.

The restaurant itself featured a well-swept, cracked cement floor painted several years ago, an old piano with missing keys tucked in the corner, and basic American food, mostly breakfasts and dinners. On other days, I came and sat at the bar and enjoyed a cup of papaya mint herbal tea served to me, when the waitress felt like it, in an old, chipped tea pot made of English everyday stoneware with a pattern all over it. A visit to the Inn was like time travel backwards. The walls in the dining area were lined with display shelves. Old plates stood on edge, showing off their design. A cracked crock, a handsome iron teapot and some sort of kitchen utensil filled out the display. Old studio photos of unidentified individuals or family groups hung on the walls.

"That's Robinson Jeffers," Paul pointed to a profile shot outdoors on a hill. Jeffers' poems about nature and God spoke to me; his notion that man was a blight on this landscape was less compelling. Jeffers wrote: *Men suffer want and become /Curiously ignoble; as prosperity/ Made them curiously vile/ But look how noble the world is...*

Heeding such words, Paul and I earnestly unloaded our lives to lessen our impact on the earth, eschewed owning a car and created virtually no trash. We felt at home in this unvarnished world.

I barely noticed the older man seated by the opposite door, very upright with his back against the chair and his knees spread wide apart. He took up a lot of space. His knit gray cardigan was busted out at the elbows; his loose woolen pants were worn but intact. He didn't have a beard, but he hadn't shaved either. A matted-haired sheep dog lay tuckered out at his feet. Or maybe the dog was just old, too. A long-haired woman stood in front of him, chest caved inward, obviously distressed. As her young voice rose, she began to gesture broadly. He cut her short – rudely, I thought - and stood up faster than I expected. He declared loudly, "Out! Out! " He looked around. "Everyone out!" I reacted as in a movie theatre. Detached. How could he kick us out? This was a public place. We continued to sit. He looked pointedly at us. Out!

We stood up, and I protested, "We haven't paid yet…"

"Out!" his voice commanded. The only other couple in the restaurant scampered out the closest door toward the front of the Inn. Our waitress loudly locked up behind them, then stayed put behind the bar, looking everywhere but at this seeming maniac. The kitchen staff disappeared. Slowly our reality sank in. This explosive old guy was the Innkeeper, known for his temper. Our delightful afternoon excursion turned sour. We might never get to return to this inn; we'd made it to his shit list through sheer bad timing.

A raft of emotions flooded over me. Shame. I've done something wrong though I didn't know what. Indignation. How could he? But most of all, I was curious. So, this was Grandpa Deetjen, friend to Robinson Jeffers, long time local, and definitely an edgy character. I'd noticed the Inn grounds were lined with wine jugs — in the garden, holding up a bank, and a half drunk one sat on a sideboard. Deetjens' didn't sell wine, didn't have the necessary permit, making it easy to give it away or enjoy a glass mid-day. Grandpa was famous for hiring hitchhikers or young women on the run. Almost everyone I met had worked a stint at the Inn. Now that I saw Grandpa in action, I knew why. He wasn't the easiest guy to work for. Some employees left, some people were fired. I made a note to never apply for a job here.

In spite of this angry man at the helm, the cohesive character of the Inn's weather-bleached siding echoed, "Time will pass but we will prevail." Maybe it was the bend in Route One, where the roadbed cut our speed dead center in front of the rustic Inn bedecked with flowers, inhaled this sight from the past, and then rounded sharply over the Castro creek bridge. A few staff stayed on permanently. Grandpa himself tinkered with the cabins, reinforcing his hand-built architecture. Workers whose reticence made it impossible for them to live in a town or in any sort of relationship hung on, as baker or carpenter. Grandpa recognized them as fellow travelers. They, in turn, worked day in and day out, wanting no other life, grateful to be here. They kept the place going. Now, he frowned deeply, his piercing blue eyes looking directly at us.

We exited out the side door directly in front of him, keeping one eye on this volcano. As soon as we left, I saw him limp into the kitchen, upright and calm, dog at his heels. At other times and places in Big Sur, I would witness similar explosions, all by self-reliant landlords, men and women of local notoriety. Although I'd lived and worked in New York City's ghettos, I'd never experienced such loud cantankerous yelling. As a means of clearing out unwelcome guests or tenants, it worked. Paul and I fast-stepped a decent distance away from the Inn, pausing on a Route One pull-out to the South. I sat on an upended boulder and Paul paced nearby. He smiled ruefully. "Well, we met Grandpa Deetjen all right." He seemed calm in the aftermath of this emotional explosion. Maybe he recognized its alcohol-fueled yelling, or maybe he just didn't care how others perceived him.

I, on the other hand, was confused, dismayed, and just plain didn't get it. I twisted my legs together to gain a better seat on my boulder. It would take me a while to realize that this force of character was part of the Big Sur frontier skill set. No one else was going to handle this or any other situation for you. The local sheriff was hours away. If pushed, you became the authority. Like the incident with the rancher on the Castro Ranch across the road, the locals were hard-pressed to know what to make of the influx of paisley-clad hitch-hikers and VW van dwellers arriving from the North and the South. We seemed like free loaders, begging for a place to unfurl a stained sleeping bag, or sit for an hour and a half over one piece of apple pie. Grandpa probably noticed that I'd quickly washed my dirty blonde hair in the convenient Inn bathroom with warm running water.

They needn't worry. The incoming winter would sweep the highway clean of the flower children, sending them packing into a few old mining cabins up Willow creek, or to rent a room in desperation from the notorious landlords who lived off their tenants housed in leaky goat sheds converted to studios. We'd be out of their hair soon enough. But on this particular day, that wasn't nearly soon enough for Grandpa, so he took matters into his own hands. We made careful note to tread softly here. The pie, though. We'd be back for more.

A Rescue From Too High

Monterey's plainspoken Alvarado Street keeps secret its many courtyards, adobe-walled gardens, and crumbing low-ceiling bars sourced from its Spanish colonial roots. This was our closest town and today's destination for supplies. Arthur's health food store sat on one of these back alleys, conveniently pushed up against an ancient thick-walled bar. We waved at a familiar Big Sur face through the small-paned bar window, and I shoved open its hefty wooden door. I wanted to pick up energy-packed buckwheat groats to sprinkle on top of our brown rice. "Get some more of those manuka raisins, too, hon," added Paul, as he sauntered down the alley to roll a cigarette for the ride back to Sur. He saluted an on-coming pedestrian.

Arthur's predated the back-to-nature health food stores of Southern California. The shop bristled boutique, with all manner of crisply boxed herb teas, vitamins for enhanced passion, and a refrigerator full of carrots to go with the pricy juicer. At Arthur's, you paid with cash and you also paid by listening to him talk for hours. Health, high colonics, and the "she's a bitch," to describe the other health food store owner in town were ladled out in his theatrical tones. I didn't know much about gay men, but there was certainly something fastidiously different about him. No wonder Paul steered clear of his verbal flood. I looked at his plump build and wondered at this intersection of health and pomposity. Tossing my three dollars on the counter, I waved a good-bye and left him mid-sentence. I would see him later waiting for a friend outside the nearby Clock restaurant.

Our outstretched thumbs caught a funky grey van with three people already in it, but we took the ride anyway. "We're just going to the beach," explained the driver, so we hopped out just fifteen minutes later. Now we carried two shopping bags and the wind was blowing in off Monastery Beach. No nuns walked its shoreline today. Paul lit up that cigarette, and I hunted for my sweater. A white swirl of fog drifted toward us off the Bay. Any ride would look good now, and so we jumped into the next car that stopped, another battered American station wagon. "Hey," grinned the driver. I should have recognized that LSD induced giddiness. I sat in the back next to a dark young man who said very little, and Paul took the front passenger seat. The driver breezed through the Carmel highlands, slowing and then picking up speed, then slowing again. His uneven pace kept me on high alert. When he hit the curves of Route One southbound, he overcorrected and then swung back on the road. "Wow!" he exclaimed several times, as if in wide-eyed awe. The sudden crunch of gravel under the tires jolted us upright, and he swung the steering wheel to the left. "That was close," breathed the now-tense man next to me, his fingers clasped tight to the arm rest.

"Yeah, sure was," the driver agreed, turning fully in his seat to look at us. "I'd be worried if I were driving this car." Huh? If he wasn't driving it then...another pebble crunch, faster. The guard rail was racing toward us. Paul reached across and rotated the top of the steering wheel, sending it back onto the road. "Wheee!" said the driver, gleefully.

"Pull off, man," said Paul in a gentle but firm voice. "We're getting out right here." The driver grinned at this new game and slammed on the brakes. I grabbed for the groceries and we leapt from the car. The driver looked upset at our departure, his playmates gone. It all happened so fast I couldn't think. A moment later, we were in a truck that had pulled over just as the wagon averted going over the edge.

"What a jerk!" pronounced our new muscular driver. "He nearly drove your whole carful of people right off over the edge. He shouldn't be driving." He shook his head in disgust. I nodded, still shaky. We were in full agreement there. My new concern was the firearm handily tucked behind the seat next to me. It wasn't dusty. "I'm Jan Brewer," our new driver introduced. Broad shouldered, blue eyes and unshaven in faded denim ranch clothes, he was our rescuer. He smiled over at us, and both Paul and I nodded, the kind of nod that encompasses a whole range of experience and puts closure on it. I smiled then with a deep sense of relief. We would later learn that he was a heavy on the Big Sur scene, ready to evict a tenant at gunpoint for a wrong no one understood. Rumor said he'd been a mercenary soldier who'd done ok. He purchased a hillside of Big Sur land and stood guard over the access to a local public beach. Every car paid. For now, his bravado calmed down our adrenaline. He could handle anything. He ranted on about hippies, and dropped us off at Nepenthe, an easy hop. Our free life on the open road came with hiccups.

At Home in a Tree

Esalen sent word they wanted Paul to come back to his old gig as gate guard. Our exile was over. Just like that, we were back at Esalen, installed in our secret camping spot next to the rock. We fit right in, old-timers now in an everchanging community of VW vans, college kids dropping out after a mind-blowing acid trip, newly split couples, and a few silently stoned Vietnam Vets. This morning the air smelled of spice, the scent of chaparral and sage releasing their oils as they gasped for water at the end of a parched summer. We shook the dew off our bedroll before stashing it in the bushes. I shivered and looked for my heavy orange cotton sweater, left over from NYC. We joined the other staff sitting on the grass in front of the office, steaming coffee mugs in hand.

"We're moving on," announced Will, one of Paul's co-workers. I sipped my coffee. No big deal. Every day somebody came or went and while I enjoyed Will and liked his old lady, Mary, we weren't close. I knew she'd miscarried a few weeks ago. "I'm going back to school, to Berkeley," he continued. "Mary and I are going to find a pad up there. So, our camping spot's up for grabs."

"Hey, I'll take it" exclaimed the newest hire in the kitchen. I hadn't caught his name, something like Raven. His dark hair spilled down his back, loose over his white Mexican shirt and his guitar case sat nearby. Sure, he needed a place. But...I couldn't finish my thought. Paul and I were fellow travelers by day and lovers by night. I'd met him on the street and that life seemed to suit him fine. A place? It was a caretaking gig. That's all we knew. But we'd been here longer, I thought, defensively.

"You'll have to talk to McElroy." continued Will. "He bought that land from one of the Murphys' and he wants a caretaker to watch over it. Maybe seventy acres, maybe forty-five, depends how you measure it from the crow's view or on the land. No pay, but you've got a spot." I looked beyond Will to his truck with built-up sides and plywood roof, a rustic camper at best. Had that camper been their home all summer?

"Where is it? asked Paul casually.

Will pointed to the hill – a mountain really – that lay just over his shoulder, a high rise to the northeast of Hot Springs Creek that butted into the Santa Lucia range. I could see a pencil-thin road gashing its way across the southern face far above us. "Close." said Will. It didn't look close to me.

"How do I find him, what does he look like?" pressed the man whose name might be Raven.

"He's here with his Italian wife. She's a talker. They're in a gray Mercedes and should be coming on property today. But I don't know when." Will sat back, tired. It probably hadn't been an easy decision for him and Mary to leave this paradise. Maybe they wanted a real home. Apparently the McElroys had easy access to Esalen as one of the neighbors. All the gate guards knew them. Now Will and Mary were giving away a spot that others would fight over.

Paul stood up, bored with the subject, I thought. "Hey Babe, let's get going," He reached out his hand and pulled me up. "Heading North." Well. That was more direction that we usually had.

At the top of the Esalen hill, we hit Route One and stuck out our thumbs pointing north, facing the few oncoming cars. Just then a young boy, maybe seventeen, appeared, walking toward us. With short stringy blonde hair and bare-faced, he carried only a small pack and his clothes were dusty with a patch of dried mud on his knees. One shoe was untied. "Hey man…," he began, the usual plea.

"You look like you've come a long way. Have some water." Paul pulled out his dented water canteen, and the boy drank it all. "Take this, too," said Paul, and passed him a handful of trail mix, our favorite cashews and raisins concoction. Then he looked him in the eye and asked, "You got any acid?"

"Yeah," said the boy. I stepped back, surprised by the change of events. "It's pure Owsley, I got it from a really close source. You want some?" Before we could respond, he reached into the front zipper pocket of his pack and pulled out a small jeweled pillbox. It sprung open easily and in it were multiple little red squares of paper. I looked at the blotter paper and recognized it. The real deal.

"Sure, man," said Paul. He reached out his palm and received the two small squares. "Later, baby," he smiled, with a wink at me. He carefully wrapped them in a small piece of cigarette paper and stuffed it into his jacket pocket. "Thank you!" He nodded his head, adding, "If you go down this hill," gesturing to the Esalen driveway, "Tell 'em Paul sent you. They'll let you into the hot baths. Looks like you could use one." We parted company.

The first car to come along didn't pick us up. Neither did the next three. Paul didn't want to stand in one place and wait, so by the time a car finally stopped we'd walked a mile north. "Where to?" hailed the driver, a single guy in his forties, American car, just driving through and hoping to get a taste of the so-called hippie movement by giving us a lift.

"Nepenthe," said Paul. It was about two pm by this time, so prime afternoon viewing on the terrace.

After some pointed questions about drugs and free love, our driver let us off in the Nepenthe parking lot, with, "Maybe I'll stop and have something to eat, too." He drove away to park. We strolled up the winding entryway between pointy succulents and red geraniums.

"Hi there!" Paul sang forth to the couple coming down. Who were they? Nice casual clothing, fit, about forty years old. Not many clues. "Hi Bob, Hi Anna Maria, nice to see you. I hear you're looking for a caretaker. I don't have wheels, but I'm a gate-guard at Esalen and we," now looking at me, "could help you out. I'm Paul. This is Brits." His nickname for me. He corrected it, "Brita." The landowners! What was going on here? Did he want us to get that caretaking place? My mind whirled.

Bob gave him a quick look over, took in his angular face, sprightly walk, and clear eyes. "I've seen you down at the Institute. Yeah." Bob was clearly surprised by our sudden appearance in his quiet afternoon. He stood awkwardly.

Anna-Maria, however, had a ready answer. "Sure, come on up and we'll talk about it. Tonight?"

"Deal!" said Paul. Luckily, he stopped short of ranting about people with Mercedes. We proceeded up to the Nepenthe deck, claiming our spot on the top row of the cement risers overlooking the guest traffic, the canyon, and the fuzzy haze over the ocean. Paul squeezed my hand. "Hey baby. We can move out of the bushes." He inhaled deeply. "Let's take that acid." The day already had me bouncing around, from no housing and a travel companion relationship to a live-together-in-these-hills, rent-free dream. Why not take a little acid to round it out?

"Sure." I sucked on the blotter paper he handed me. Nothing happened. Maybe it was fake. Then slowly the colors of the ocean took on an extra depth and I could hear the waves pounding against a boulder far away, down the coast. The hills began to undulate, and Paul's face resembled an old Indian. Just sitting here, breathing, was enough. The warmth of the sun, the glass of water handed me by a waiter we knew, and Paul's presence next to me blended into a warm haze. The sun began its descent into afternoon and my shadow lengthened. I watched it, wondering about our relationship, my shadow and me.

Paul interrupted my musings. He stood up and bounded down the risers. I stood slowly, swaying for a second before I gained my upright stance. I cautiously stepped down, aware that my body felt fluid and unstable. Taking a deep breath, my bones became solid again, and we walked between the fragrant geraniums back to the road. "Let's catch the next ride," said Paul, swinging his arm out and following through with his torso and legs to pantomime netting a car. I laughed and laughed. What a perfect day. Sure enough, the next car pulled over. I just kept laughing. Paul was my universe for now.

Our ride let us out just north of the Hot Springs Bridge. As usual, Paul didn't let on exactly where we were going. Where we were actually going today was up to check on our new digs and cement the deal.

In the manner that psychedelics can induce, I recovered from my fluid legs and became an able hiker. We strolled the relatively flat entry driveway. I barely noticed the steep walk beyond to an even stronger sage fragrance. The rocks seemed to be talking to me. We were so high! Hot Springs Creek sang its lilting tune far below. We came to a bend and the scent of bay trees overwhelmed everything else. The road opened onto a recently excavated clearing, a ledge about thirty feet across. There were no structures, just dirt. I could see what might be a tent lying neatly wrapped on the ground. Maybe they slept outside too. Bob and Anna-Maria were gathered around a small fire fitted with a real grill. A halved buoy encircled the flames nicely. Psychedelics take away my appetite, so I politely declined their offer of pasta carbonara. Anna Maria recited the recipe for me. "Just make pasta, drain the liquid reserving a little, add a beaten egg, stir, add a dollop of olive oil of course." She paused and smiled, tossing the pasta carefully with a fork. then went on. "Shake in lots of Parmesan cheese. Delicious!" She sprinkled chopped parsley on the top. I had to agree, it looked yummy. When Anna Maria parsed a pear lengthwise for dessert, my eyes grew big and I burst out, "I've never seen such a beautiful fruit!" She was completely unfazed by my enthusiasm.

"Yes...!" and with that she launched into a tale in her singsong accent about her aunt in Italy and a lover and a mysterious fruit on a pear tree. Stoned as I was, I could follow her energy but not the story. I laughed delightedly. Within an hour we had the gig. Paul and Bob stayed quiet, a communal silence in the force-field of this attractive and sharp-tongued woman. We scheduled our move-in date for two weeks hence, right after they departed to their home in Pennsylvania's tony suburbs where he had clients waiting for his clean-lined house designs. They'd be back in mid-winter. Or spring. He gave us his address and phone number and described his contacts in the neighborhood. Tall Paul, another architect, and Joe Koeyman, a noted gardener and self-trained builder, would both be able to contact him. They lived nearby.

An avid backpacker, he'd met Anna Maria as a serviceman in post-war Northern Italy. They seemed less than ideally suited to each other, I thought. Yet her vibrancy buoyed his deep pragmatism and they both loved outdoor living. They had three daughters, and we'd meet them next trip. We somehow became part of their plan to live in nature. With trim bodies and short hair, they wore their outdoor flannel comfortably. Her hiking boots somehow looked chic. She showed us the hiking stick she'd collected in the woods that morning.

"Oh," Bob added as an afterthought. "By the time you get here, this tree platform will be finished. Our tools will be in the lockers that make up the edging, but I'll leave a couple empty for you." It was nearly dark now, but I could see three planks lying across the edgy bay tree. I looked down. The hill descended into darkness. I had no idea how far the canyon dropped below the treehouse; I guess I'll see in the daylight. Tree platform? Bob was an architect, and every so often he met up with Steward Brand, the geodesic dome guy, who shared his admiration for lighter structures. So, Paul and I would share a home built not on land but on air. In my altered state of mind, these were all the details I needed.

We danced our way down the hill. The man whose name might be Raven looked crestfallen at our news. I coined an adage to myself that kept me in good stead during my following fifty years in Big Sur: "All's fair in love and Big Sur housing."

WHERE GIANTS PLAY

Thanks, man! Paul tipped his imaginary hat to the long-haired young driver of the dented Ford Econoline van. Moving day. We spilled out the rear door, landing on the dirt shoulder of snaky Route One. I dusted off my woven shoulder bag, hoisted my sleeping gear, grabbed my orange duffle, and then took a closer look at the rocky driveway jutting off in a lazy easterly fashion. A loose-padlocked chain hung between two spindly pines marking its entrance. This had to be the place, our new place. We'd been here once before. I neatly stepped over the chain, Paul following, slightly bent over with the weight of our food bag as well as his backpack. We locked eyes and grinned. Mission accomplished. Our ride from Monterey had been easy and we should be asleep under the stars before long.

    I'd already learned to double check Paul when it came to distance or time. He wanted to holler from the top of every mountain and laughed when he fell into the creek. I never saw him tire or even sweat. As for me, I panted a few steps behind with what to me were very reasonable thoughts running through my head: Is this the right way? I hadn't paid any attention on our initial visit. Is the roadbed stable or will we slide back down? What about water? Will I survive this journey? Today, I would learn a new concept: elevation. I squirmed a pebble out of my left sandal. The narrow driveway started out flat, sashaying between chaparral, greasewood, and sage. It looked freshly bulldozed, with loose-flung clods of dirt and rocks masking any indication of recent tire treads. An inviting rock grotto to the left opened onto a small flat of dead grasses. I was surprised to see bee hives stacked in a neat row with an active buzzing encircling them. We didn't stop. A minute more and the innermost embankment showed a fifteen-foot high earthen cut, with tumbling rock and sprouting sagebrush indicating that this was a new pathway into the interior of Big Sur, not an old ranch trail. I could hear the fluid gush of Hot Springs creek below. Below! That would be a three hundred foot drop. Not even a deer path crossed through that thicket of tangled deadwood and sliding granite. My stomach caught at the precariousness of our soon-to-be perch. Don't even think about it, I advised myself. As long as I looked straight ahead, it didn't matter.

We walked on. Paul led like a pent-up pony on the loose. I inwardly groaned. The road snaked to the right again, seemingly aimlessly. I stumbled and steadied my gear as the sharp assent began. I looked up to a hairpin curve. Could that be our destination? I tentatively raised my eyes and saw, high above me, a sliver of this same road making an easy run across the western face of the hillside. Then it too disappeared, presumably to lead upward, high across the Hot Springs canyon wall. How much farther? Paul was way ahead of me now. Even though I knew it was silly, I didn't like hiking alone. I feared coyotes and worse. I picked up my tired feet, slick in handmade leather sandals, and increased my pace.

The road squirming across the canyon wall was a welcome relief from the previous 45° degree upward slant. The deep cut allowed just enough width for a single car to pass this way. I marveled at the men who had come before and scrapped it out with their small bulldozers. "Who built this?" I would ask. It turned out to be the last Big Sur road designed by the dozer operator. Earlier that summer at another site he accidentally killed his teen son under a load of dirt. Grief stricken, he finished up his contracts, turned off his heavy machinery and left town. This nasty scrap of road against the hillside reflected his loss. I stopped again and took a sip of water from my tin army canteen. I dropped the heavy sleeping roll, planning to hike back and pick it up. The upside of the road seemed straight-up steep. I could see tumbled rocks above me waiting to complete their journey. Instinctively I covered my head with my hands.

Higher up stretched more chaparral and scrub. Small wild lilac trees grew in an irregular pattern, interrupted by deadwood. Known locally as tick trees, this cyanosis lives about 40 years and then dies, leaving a scrappy sharp hardwood. I surveyed the hillside and saw very little green, just many bushes starved for thirst. No rain fell during the coastal summer, so today everything was dry, brown, crackly. I will admit at times like this, I openly prayed to whatever holy spirit still remained with me, "Help get me through just this one more mountainous trail without stumbling!" By winter's end this country would make a believer of me, a believer in spirit here and everywhere, a believer in help and in the wonders of coincidence when nothing else would work. I took another sip of water. The road lay straight and empty before me.

With a lighter load, I could walk faster. I was just getting into the swing of it when the road turned sharply left. "Hey Baby!" Paul ran toward me, arms outstretched, hugging me broadly. "This is it!" I gazed around, taking in the even deeper cut that created a flat ledge in the hill, about thirty feet across. We were now on the backside of the first range of hills, with another range of the Santa Lucia Mountains rising eastward. To my left the deep cut continued its rise to more mountain. Straight ahead the road dead-ended in an oak and redwood forest bound further by a canyon wall hollowed by a chilly, spring-fed tributary of Hot Springs creek. To my right on the east side was that drop of canyon. "Ahoy!" shouted Paul. We laughed to hear the echo return from four directions.

A slick green California bay tree had rooted itself about thirty feet down the slope, spilling its spicy scent over us. True to his word, Bob MacElroy had laid twenty freshly purchased boards across the thick tree limbs to form a smooth platform. A few boards lay perpendicular to it, creating a level gangplank. I walked directly across the gangplank to the loose platform. It is the nature of trees to sway, and this tree was no exception. I swayed as I crossed the gangplank. We felt the tree swoosh and sway when we lay down. Our vestigial arboreal nature loved the sway, the heights. Had humankind descended from primates playing in the tree tops? We would live and play in this tree for the next season. My feet lightly flew down the road as I backtracked to retrieve the bedroll. I carefully carried it over the gangplank, spread it out, and sank gratefully into our newest leaf-roofed bedroom.

Minutes later, I heard Paul whistle. "You won't believe this!" When I didn't stir, he persisted, "You got to see it. " So I rose, mindful of the drop from the gangplank to the hillside. Sleepily I walked to the back rim of the ledge toward the forest. I didn't see anything. I tried to look interested. Paul pointed up the shadowy hillside. My eyes adjusted. I could make out a big rock. "So what?" I grouched. Then my eyes grew accustomed to the shadows and I could see the rocky cairn he was referring to. Maybe giants had played rock toss in these mountains. Just above us rested two car-sized boulders spaced about six feet apart. Between them another equal sized boulder had tumbled down, coming to rest balanced in the middle. I stepped back in alarm. It looked for all the world as if it could continue its tumble and roll rapidly toward me in a second.

Noting my response, Paul assured me, "They've probably sat like that for hundreds of years." Maybe. Big Sur taught me that anything can roll at any moment. Love nature but keep an eye on it. Still, this was too good. We unpacked the flashlight and skidded through the leafy debris up the small rise to the rocky catch. The area under the rocks smelled of animals and urine, although our light beam caught only a whitened skeletal rat's skull, no other bones left. I could see there was enough space to crawl into the box-sized hollow under the rocks. No thanks. This rock catchment was a visible sign of the whimsical nature of these hills, the chance to live wild and free-rolling, equally balanced by the chance to stumble toward a long fall. Or be smashed.

The site was so remarkable, and hidden in shadows, that I can find no photo evidence of it. Yet I know it was there. Five years later the next mountain caretaker blasted it out. I was astonished that he could destroy such a geologic miracle. "It was too dangerous for my wife and child to live under," he neatly explained.

Dawn offered the best lightshow of the day when the sun rose above the Eastern range, its rays lengthening to brighten redwoods spires, send shadows across granite slabs pushed upward from the sub strata, and illuminate the south facade of the canyon. This morning Paul stirred enough embers from last night's enclosed fire bed to spark it back to life. He grasped and unplugged the narrow black plastic hose, its end anchored hundreds of feet away in a small spring, and filled the blue graniteware coffee pot to boil water. He added the coffee grounds, and we waited while they lazily settled to the bottom. No filter. Camp coffee. I carefully poured myself a fragrant cup. I gripped the metal mug with both hands to warm up, rousting the morning chill.

Fog rose in shaggy streamers from the canyon bed. This deep canyon, high hills, bright sun over foggy underlay, defined the central coast as a land of extremes. The Santa Lucia Mountains rise in a subduction plate lifting directly out of the Pacific. The decomposing granite gives a fairly stable base, and higher up, solid rock cliffs soar. This is the steepest mountain range in the continental United states. The hills ascend 2,000 feet, pause, and then rise 2000 feet and even more, descending eastwardly in a grassy sprawl toward old turn-of-the-century cattle ranches and eventually the Salinas Valley. That side was history territory.

On this western side, early white explorers had a harder time with the steep reaches from the coast or stretching through non-existent passes from the Valley. If they conquered the ridgeline, the slippery mountains fought their every dream and the rocky coast thwarted their ships. Only the pirates enjoyed the hidden coves with entrance accessible at high tide when the rocks were deep underwater. No doubt the indigenous folk were smiling as they annually moved inland from the coast.

The photo shows me in a later shack at this site. Even after few months into our new digs – literally, since our home landing pad was a freshly dug earthen cut into the hillside – I never rested easy in these hills. My dreams opened onto dark characters appearing suddenly out of the high oak and redwood forests.

Almost every other word here rhymed with edge. I cannot say I ever came to a peace treaty with this country. Yet as it took my breath away it grabbed my heartstrings. When my old college friend Katie King visited, she nailed it. "It's fucking steep here in Big Sur."

Where Giants Play

The Edgy Canyon of Natural Love

The tree platform swayed as I shifted my weight. I steadied myself. Paul and I were going to live in a tree, like early native peoples. This tree. Rock-a-bye baby! Why shouldn't we? The land dropped twenty-five feet down the mountain on the outside edge of the plank flooring, and nothing but gravity anchored it to the native Bay tree limbs lifting it from below. Like us, it was free to move, to shake, and no one had ever tried this design in a high wind. The inner margin of the platform almost hugged the hillside, except the builder ended up a few boards short. He positioned a gangplank over this shortfall, and it was on this narrow board I gingerly walked, carrying my duffle of laundry and a pillow found in the Free Box.

"Feel this!" grinned Paul, standing wide-legged, setting it rocking even more. Safety was not his concern. He liked to create things; he hated boxes. I was beginning to realize that an actual house would be way over his top. This open-air site suited him, and it suited the person I was turning into. He danced around the deck, plucked leaves and tucked them behind my ears. The breeze blew my dress, and I invited its airy puffs to twirl me around as it rustled through the treetops. He looked out over the deeply grooved Hot Springs canyon dropping hundreds of feet down to the creek, and the mountains looming high beyond raw hills.

"Halloo!" he yelled out, listening to his voice pirouette down into the valley and echo back. He sang loudly, "On a clear day…rise and look around you…and see where you are…" His theme. His voice rang across the canyon gulf to a pale rock-faced cliffside on the Eastern slope. Later we would see hikers descend to that white cliff drop and holler out for help as they sought to scramble back up the path. This land suited Gods, wild animals, and owls. Man had to make his own way. "Makes you strong or breaks you," as the local lore went.

This was our place. I breathed it in. The absentee landowners from Pennsylvania had chosen us as caretakers, to watch over these hills and make sure no citified hikers set fires or moved in their own camps. In the process, we'd defined ourselves as a couple. Or so I thought. Yes, I had a husband elsewhere, but he had a girlfriend, and it was time we cut the thread. I'd do that, soon, next trip back to the city.

I lay down on the new bed and gazed up into the branches. We'd upgraded to an abandoned 4-inch Posturepedic mattress after our lumpy campsite. I sat up, slipped off my cotton dress, and nestled my naked body into the covers. Paul removed his loose boots, his old cords, his trademark red sweater, and joined me, wrapping his arms and legs around my body in a tight embrace, no rush. "We did it, baby", he breathed. "We're here." The shadows turned to darkness and the embrace loosened to sensual caresses, deep gasps of breath, exhaled ohs and ahs. The popular new photo book **Kama Sutra** enrolled us in an erotic spiritual practice. Tonight Paul encouraged me into an active position, letting me take more control of our passion. We coaxed, moaned, and let loose uninhibited cries of release. Later he whispered, "Baby I love you", yet I was so relaxed and so drowsy I wasn't sure he really said it. The stars dropped down all around us. We were alone on our mountain.

Our spot lost the sun to the western side of the hill at two pm. Yet I could still see sunlight shining on the opposite side of Hot Springs Canyon. Its warmth and brightness called me away from my lunchtime cheese sandwich. Everything down the hill seemed bathed in light, or maybe it was my post LSD trip. "Hey Paul," I smiled. "Let's go to Monterey. We're almost out of candles." So, we skipped down the mountain driveway and set out. But rides were slow and we only got halfway there, to Palo Colorado. The wind came up. We turned back. With ten dollars still in my pocket, our ride let us out at Redwood grocery, where I purchased a few candles, cold cuts, and a bottle of wine.

The bar was right next door. "Hey!" and we swung open the heavy wood door. Dusty Christmas lights hung unstrung on one wall and a covey of men in cowboy hats crowded over the bar, telling the tall tales Big Sur locals are famous for, and punching each other's shoulders when a particularly outrageous act was described well. They already knew most of the stories. There were no empty stools, so I stood by while Paul tossed back a beer and occasionally commented on a tale, I looked up when the bar door swung open and in walked Millie from the Esalen Office. Usually cool and aloof, closer to Paul in age, she surprised me with a wide smile and spritely greeting. Maybe she'd had a drink, too. She had two names, Amy and Janie. Tonight, she was Amy. Her dyed ruddy hair and lipstick seemed at home here. Her body was trim, her eyes tired. The bartender poured her favorite amber-colored drink without her asking.

"My cabin's right here. Come on by," Amy invited, her eyes crinkling in a smile. Redwood Bar was perhaps the oldest of the Big Sur hangouts with a history that encompassed Esalen psychologist Joe Adams as owner, the Berkeley Sexual Freedom league for their annual getaway, and a Hells Angels roust by locals. Word had it that the front door was often locked, leaving the back entry for those in the know. Of course I wanted to stop by, see more of this funky resort. We left by the back door and followed Amy down a winding dirt path through the gloom to reach her redwood cabin. I was so wrapped up in the legends of the place that I didn't pay attention to Paul, to Amy, to the pathway. Once inside her one room cabin, she stood in the kitchen area, I sat on the bed, and Paul lounged back in the sole chair, cozy.

Like Paul, she was from LA and acquainted with many of the Esalen staff from their pre-drop-out city days. Soon she was telling us about her life as a well-paid "call girl named Janie," a profession she was determined to leave. All those dates sounded like prostitution to me. She justified, "Why not? It was fun. I needed the cash after my car was hit, and the next thing I knew...well, there I was. But some weird shit came down, I almost got really injured." I felt my judgment rise, close me down. Relationships for money dishonored sex in my mind. I grew quiet. The walls closed in on me. This evening was not going well. "I had to get out of the city, so toxic," she explained. Then she looked wistful as she added, "I never had any real trouble though." I sensed that this forty-two-year-old woman had enjoyed the high ride and now felt old, over the hill. She came to Big Sur to re-boot but wasn't sure how. She looked away and steeled her jaw. I looked at her worn face, clipped wavy hair, widening waist, and brassiere-supported breasts and I didn't see a lot of sexuality. The glow had definitely worn off. She dropped her businesslike speech and became more vulnerable. "I came up here to clean up, get a real relationship." Her brow smoothed and her eyes looked hopeful, mouth serious.

We shared our wine and cold cuts. We drank a second bottle she uncorked, and she politely put out crackers and cheese. Soon that bottle was empty. "Hey, got another one?" Paul demanded in a loud voice. I stood up, unsteady. I'd had enough. Amy poked under her sink and obligingly pulled her last bottle out. Paul smiled and proceeded to drink most of it. He jumped up and drew us into a western bar shoot-em-up scene he'd played in "Bonanza". His voice deepened, changed, and he started yelling about a director who'd flubbed the scene. "Can't go back to Hollywood, they're all crazy!" he exploded, louder. Annoyed by his outburst, I tried to sooth his confrontational mood, laughing with him at those crazy Hollywood types. Next minute, he was yelling at me for interrupting. I slumped down.

He stood up, legs spread. He looked around the tidy cabin and his voice rose a decibel. "Fucking motel owners just catering to the tourists with no regard for us locals, the folks who live here, make the place what it is. Did you hear the music in there! Stinking! Johnny plays a better drum. Hell, Big Sur ought to go back to the Indians. Nobody owns the fucking land but God!" He smiled. "Or Goddess." He grew louder, gesturing and taking on an oratorical tone. "And this" he held up the last of the joint, "will save us, get us back in touch with Spirit...far in, not far out!" he proclaimed, in spite of now being more drunk than stoned.

Amy joked along at first. As he lashed loudly onward, she turned her back and squirted detergent over the sinkful of dishes. Paul paced the room, tossing his shoulders, and now lambasting the locals for building the road through these wild mountains, "this unspoiled land," the very road we'd just hitch hiked up to get here. I wrapped my arms around myself, scared by this rapid change of mood and wondered why Amy didn't say something. It didn't occur to me to say something. He might get madder. He pointed his finger at Amy. "And you. You can be forgiven for selling your body for sex." She looked sick. "But what are you doing sitting in an office up here at Esalen when that's what you left down south!" He careened into a table lamp and sent it tilting toward the floor but remarkably he retrieved it at the last minute, denting its shade. He looked at it and dented the shade more. "That's better. Hate anything that's perfect." He laughed at his joke.

"Well, Paul," Amy interrupted him, slowly, deliberately. She straightened up. She smiled, officious. "Party's over. I've got to work tomorrow. Why don't you forget about hitching south and sleep on the outside bed? Take off at first light." For a minute Paul looked as If he would challenge her for killing his rant, but then he snapped on his cowboy hat, tipped it at her, bowed deeply to me with a flourish toward the door and stepped out. I turned to Amy and made a face. I knew we'd overstepped our welcome and my polite upbringing was shamed by this too loud, too mocking tirade. She held her ground. "Night."

My stomach tightened; my body hurt. This was my new lover, my guy. We were living the natural life, just the way everyone dreamed. What was happening? Paul raged on. Blood pounded in my ears. I was scared of his rage and I was scared he was leaving me, both at the same time.

Once outside, he stomped off in the other direction. The redwoods sighed high above, their tips cutting the stars. I could hear Paul wind his way upstream, his energy gunning his pace. My mind reeled as I sought to take in the events of the evening and fit them into the Paul I thought I knew, the man with whom I'd spent the last three months sharing the stars, sleeping in these hills, loving his in-the-moment sense of play. I scrunched my shoulders up to stay warm in the damp canyon. I needed my sweater. I sniffled, trying to forget it all. Damn! I'd blocked out his anger and had focused instead on him as play pal. Yet tonight when he leaned into his rage, the Irish Indian came out, undoing all his solitary walkabouts in the Mexican desert, and all the well-honed marijuana nirvana.

Exhausted, I sat on the log and warily listened for Paul's return. I heard rustling in the underbrush and imagined rats and night birds. A nearby camper's dog barked. The silence grew noisier. It didn't feel exactly safe here. I needed to calm my fears, take this like an adventure. I took a breath, exhaled long. Redwood Bar was a roadhouse with a wild reputation. I could hear the band wheeze out a drunken beat to inspire the last of the lonely cowboys to get a move on. The forest ground was uneven. Paul was missing. I was cold. I took another breath but rather than calm me, it augmented my panic. I couldn't quite exhale fully. The rocks in the stream created a steady splash, loud enough to make me wonder if I would ever hear him in the distance. Was he ok? He didn't usually drink, and this was the first time I'd seen him clean all the liquor out of a host's kitchen. I grew anxious as I considered all the things that could be happening to him right now. He could fall. Hit his head of a rock in the river. Or he could just take off, thumb out, pretty much how we'd met.

Paul didn't carry much baggage except what he carried in his head, his "haunted hermit." I was just beginning to become acquainted with those memories, and they weren't pretty. Could it be he was running from his demons with his love of the highway? A hint I found later, scrawled on a torn sheet of paper, "Something timid and frightened has caught me and bound me…I was afraid of the freedom to learn from people, I thought I'd find out how rotten and unfeeling I had been while pretending to be everyone's friend. I'm full of guilt and rejection and fear to be really real." His goal: "I'm sure I have creative powers that are just stagnating. I need a knowledge that my work is justifiably rewarding, not just a dollar in exchange for my time." These thoughts and a bottle of wine sent him stomping through the redwood forest, ever further away from me.

My dreams weren't as grand. I wanted to leave American's white picket fence 9-5 reality behind, in favor of a return to nature.

Steeped

But, was this it? I sank deeper into the gloomy dampness of the river bottom, head bent low, the earthy smell of needles comingling with the moist air. The thick tree trunks silently sucked the water up into the towering, shadowed redwood limbs. I shook the forest needles off a blanket and lay down on the old foam pad, this so-called outdoor sleeping platform, sans pillows.

I had just dozed off when Paul returned, looming large over my head. "So, Brita, you think you can sleep when the planet is spinning?" and with that he was off again, pacing, raging against America, against conformity, against organized religion. I sat up warily. He tilted his chin skyward. "Come and get me!" he hollered. "I'm waiting for you." He turned to me. "Those flying saucers been tracking me. I want to go, meet their people. They're coming." He paused, then bellowed, "Right here, come on down." A light flickered on in a cabin up the creek. I was sure we would be thrown out any minute. But his booming voice was outshouted by the river, creating a cacophony of sound. At last, he sat on a stump, spent. I rolled over and tried to calm myself enough to get a little rest. If this continued tomorrow, I'd need all my wits about me. No hugs tonight.

After hours of listening to small animal sounds in the thicket I opened my eyes to see the shapes of the trees appear and the land began to lighten in that hulking way that dawn arrives, solemnly. The nearby dog barked his alert. Paul smiled down at me, sidelying, head resting on his arm. "You're a great travel companion," he said gently. He stretched out on the bed. I was relieved. Scared as I was of this new personality who had emerged, I still hoped for a new day. "But we're not a couple." He went on. "We're just travel companions. After a few minutes he rose again. "I'm going now." He pulled on his worn boots, righted his knapsack on his back, and stood. He turned and started up the hillside path toward Route One. The stream flowed on. Paul moved easily in the pre-dawn.

With those words, he shot down my teen-aged notions of "love forever," replacing them with "Love today." This aligned with the Haight Street cultural motto, "free love" implying a sort of rolling bed party. Ownership was out, be it land ownership or partner ownership. Yet my body pulled inward, and my mind flew away. "No" I cried. "Don't go." He continued without looked back.

I inhaled the earthy loam smells and sneezed. It was the hour of the Wolf, as Ingmar Bergman described in his movies, the dark hour before dawn. When more people die. Nearby, the little Sur River gushed. I retrieved my jacket, found my shoes, and tried to stand, too knocked off center by this turn of events to walk. I just couldn't face Route One and jump in a stranger's car like this.

I inched my way to a smooth boulder by the creek's edge. I sat down on the hard rock, shivering, unmoored. The flowing stream coaxed my tears out, and as I cried the earth cried with me, emitting giant streams of tears. The hell of Vietnam, the emptiness of America's prosperous materialism, and my own now abandoned relationship swelled up in wet sorrow. I paused. I listened. The river was crying with me. I cried more and it joined in, dripping tears of lost love and the loss of everything I had turned toward in my flight to Big Sur, now a woman alone. I felt at one with a whole process of waters flowing. I was part of a natural cycle. I stopped crying and just sat, the seat of my pants getting soggy from the canyon bottom.

Paul returned in about half an hour. His compass always worked when it came to finding me. "I'm sorry, baby," he said, looking directly at me. "You're a great travel companion. Let's keep doing this." I smiled, relieved, and paid no attention to the back of my mind's insistent question: What was this all about? The sun rose and we could hitch home to our swaying tree platform. "On a clear day…" sang out Paul, again. The first car down the road, a ford station wagon, picked us up.

I Was the Secret In My Family

I bathed naked in the hot springs and didn't care who listened in on my side of most any phone conversation placed on the payphone. An enthusiastic crowd of eavesdroppers offered advice and made note of my every word, fodder for the gossip mill, while the dimes jangled into the phone. We knew each other's secrets.

Yet a lot of my life story went unspoken. Was I secretive? Let's just say my years of living an alternative lifestyle while finishing college and working as a fast-typing secretary (I called myself an editor) had made me adept at slipping from one reality to another. For reasons I didn't fully understand, this double reality was particularly true with my parents and my brothers, tucked away in the family home up on Vashon Island, a short ferry hop from Seattle, home to Boeing aircraft (and therefore in military alignment) and the logging industry. "Don't tell my folks." The distance helped.

This autumn morning I was on my way from my bedroll on the Big Sur earth to my grandfather's 75th birthday celebration, up on the Pacific Northwest Island farm he built in 1914. I'd found a ride to the airport and now all I had to do was pack a few clothes into my small carry-on bag. But what clothes? I rummaged through my army duffle tucked beneath a tree, and finally from the bottom corner, I pulled out a crumpled ball of sturdy lace: my bra. I located other undergarments and slipped into them, feeling the constraints of civilization, and its devaluation of the feminine body, settle over me. I couldn't breathe. Ok, I loosened the bra to its maximum width and knew I better get used to it. From a bag on the side of the duffle, I pulled out the scuffed leather shoes with the stacked heels, librarian style.

My dress looked nice enough. The loose fit skimmed my hips and floated above my knees, showing off my now-muscular legs. The peasant pattern spoke of ethnicity. I'd copied the design from a model in the Kristina Gorby shop, St. Marks place, NYC, last year. After all this hiking it hung on me now. I stopped short of pulling my long blonde hair off my neck and securing it with a barrette. I didn't want to look like Alice in Wonderland, too tidy for me. There'd be time for that at the airport. Finally, I found my eyeglasses and realized my astigmatism hadn't hampered me in months. I tucked them into my bag and set off to catch my ride north. I barely noticed the broad horizon of sea and the cypress trees highlighted by the morning sunlight.

I puzzled over my efforts to maintain this charade. While I knew my Dad, particularly, would accept me as I was, and maybe even admire me for it, I also knew that he was concerned for my secure future. This life I had fallen into promised anything but security. Nothing steady, apparently no more marriage. A defiant attitude. "You and your friends are dissidents," he declared, relieved to give us a name. To me, his kind of security meant repression, phoniness, and a cop out. I knew nothing was secure, so why pretend?

As I walked briskly through the rotating doors into SFO's row of airline agents, I straightened up. Some of my hometown neighbors from Vashon Island were pilots for Northwest Airlines. Instinctively I reached for my barrette and pinned my hair back, lest I run into anyone I knew. My small island community kept watch on my Dad's behavior thanks to his senior position at the local high school. After twenty-five years of teaching U.S. History and coaching tennis and debate, virtually every long-term island resident for one or two generations had sat in his classroom and experienced his clear blue eyes as he said with a little smile "Now number your page 1 to 10. First question: Who served as secretary of State under Woodrow Wilson?" and so on. Because of this authority, he had his detractors including a few parents who would love to point at him as the reason their son got a "C" rather than at their son himself. I knew my behavior counted in this equation. I had moved 3000 miles away to get out from under those spying eyes, then returned West to the California Coast. As the plane lifted off, I slipped on lipstick and read the *San Francisco Chronicle* to catch up.

I fell into my customary doze zone. Thoughtful. I had dropped out. I didn't live under a roof. I didn't want to. I ridiculed those who arrived at Esalen with a fistful of money claiming to be hip because they wore bell-bottoms and took LSD. With every bone in my body I tried to leave America's middle-class ethos. Yet when I went back to my hometown, I pocketed my defiance and smiled sweetly in agreement with my plump Finnish farmer grandmother when she looked up from the apples she was peeling and said, "A married woman like you shouldn't wear your hair down like that." I loved my grandmother. I feared my voice could upend my Father's highly regarded faculty career. I kept my hair tied back until I snapped my seat belt into place on my return flight back to San Francisco. Click! I shook my head to tumble down my hair and grinned. I could pull off this double life a bit longer: hippie and straight; married and single; anti-materialistic and working days in San Francisco offices; a romantic masquerading as a travel companion. What else?

Untie This Vow

Now we were really locals with our own spot. Paul stayed steady at his Esalen gig. Pay day came; he hitched to Monterey to buy a tin of tobacco. Once the sun dipped behind the hill, I skipped down to Esalen. "Someone's waiting for you in the lodge." The gate-guard's announcement stopped me in my tracks. Someone was waiting for me? Here, when no one knew where I was? My breath caught up a deep intake and was ragged as I exhaled. I enjoyed this secret life. Yet—who was this?

Only a few folks hung around the lodge during this midafternoon time. A couple of guests shared a deep conversation over tepid tea in the back corner. Near the windows Fritz Perls, clad in his grey one piece workman's uniform with a lit cigarette in his hand, sat playing chess with a staff member. Watching the game intently from across the table I spotted a man, neatly dressed in corduroy pants, boots turned slightly out, a tucked in paisley shirt, bearded. Something was familiar…I looked more closely. Bob! My husband. When I headed south, he crossed the country Eastward. Yet – I blinked – here he was, apparently alone and without Nancy, his latest girl. My head spun. At the same time, I was inexplicably happy to see him. His vibrancy filled the space and I could see even Fritz was curious. "Bob!" I exclaimed loudly.

He gave the board a last glance, rose, and greeted me with a close hug. "Baby," he murmured, tickling my ear with his tongue. Then he stood back. "Hey, I found your spot. Easy-lon. Are you enlightened yet?" he chided me loudly. "You like living out here in the sticks?" He looked around, as if to find a few more people. He liked to be where things were happening, in coffee shops and outdoor concerts. Nature didn't call to him like it did to me and to the million other American young people who would flee the city this decade, seeking serenity in country living after the drug-rattled streets of San Francisco and other urban centers. "C'mon, let's get out of here." He sang out, "Just like a rolling stone."

A few minutes later, we were at the base of my mountain, tucked into the little grotto pungent with bay, a hidden cove. The bee hives had gone off with the beekeeper. I knew Paul was away in town, yet I didn't want Bob to see our tree platform home. Way too personal. So, we spread out a blanket, hugged, kissed, exchanged travel stories. Then I pulled back.

"Hey," I said. He caught my changed tone and sat back, too, looking straight at me through those shaggy eyebrows. I waffled. I hate endings. And I loved Bob. Yet... "Bob, it's time to face it. This marriage is over. We'll always love each other, but you're with Nancy and I'm with Paul." As I said it I recognized the tenuous nature of these alternative relations. Yet their very existence threw our vows out the window.

Bob looked calm. "Yeah. Ok. Seems like it" he looked down and became silent. My face tightened with emotion. He finally said, "I feel like a rooster without its head, just flailing around." He looked up and I saw a tear. "I'll really miss you, baby." More silence. I smiled at him knowing we were ok.

We worked out a few details such as continuing to share the room in San Francisco. We had a phone there. Although our marriage was heartfelt, our actual wedding had been inspired by the far-off war in Vietnam and the early policy of not drafting married men. We didn't really believe in marriage – it was a property agreement – so we didn't really need to think about divorce. Those matters would unfold slowly.

I walked with him wordlessly in the dusk down to his car and heard his "bye Brita," and the slam of the door, the sound of the engine starting and pulling unflinchingly back onto Route One, heading North. There was no looking back.

Steal this Cheese: End the War

Sewing my own clothes was one of the ways I waged war on the up-tight social order and the ruinous industrial military complex. I wanted clothes that defined me, flowed, twirled when I walked, whispered of ethnic origins. I spent hours in Britex Fabrics in downtown San Francisco, fingering the printed velvets and the snaky synthetics. Forget the poplin, the button-up Donkenny blouse. I let my imagination run free as I saw the design possibilities. The look would be my own, the clothes would move smoothly over my body, there'd be no fitting ready-to-wear onto my lifestyle. I created my own patterns. My current design focus was on the slim A-line dress cut short at mid-thigh, with the long droopy sleeves I saw on Gracie Slick when she sang about reality dancing backward in *White Rabbit*. I selected fabric; I sewed it up.

I'd worn this new velour dress, in an orange, turquoise, and purple paisley border print, my legs wrapped with bright orange tights, at yesterday's peace rally to make a clear stand. "End the War" with the subtext, "End Profit Mongering," the cause of war. In my rush to get out of town, I'd slipped on the same outfit again today. In hindsight this wasn't the best choice. Why? You might ask. Stealing was my next favorite way of dealing with the industrial military complex.

Paul and I were in San Francisco on a supply run, gathering whatever we could fit in our duffels to haul back to our new caretaking gig. As a relic from my now-finished marriage, I still rented the backyard room of an old rooming house on Dubois Street. We sauntered down the two-blocks to the Safeway grocery store on Market Street. Paul selected a bag of walnuts and I hit the cheese section. Kuminost. I loved the caraway flavored cheese, but

Steal this Cheese: End the War

I had only ten dollars and I'd already tallied that up on absolute necessities like soap and Wesson oil, two onions, a bag of rice.

That cheese would be so good later today, I mused. Without another thought, I stood facing the cheddar selection and feigned casual as I glanced left and right and slipped the kuminost from my hand into my zipper purse. I zipped up and I took a deep breath, feeling certain no one had seen me. I loved to trick the profit-taking stores that refused food to the poor, to fool these vast banks of plump fruit and steak available only to those with funds. "Let's go, " I announced to Paul as he danced up another isle, rearranging the towers of canned goods. I checked through the line. Oddly, he glanced back at me then uncharacteristically proceeded me through the wide front doors of the store that opened onto the parking lot. I hurried to catch up. "Look...," I gloated, as I reached for the hidden cheese. He looked down and mumbled as I felt a tap on my shoulder.

"Excuse me, come with me, please." A uniformed man stood behind my left elbow. I straightened up, startled. As I turned toward him, he firmly grasped my elbow and led me back into the store. Paul walked on, head down. I felt a shaking permeate my body as the scene snapped into focus. I was busted, plain and simple. In all the demonstrations, I'd made it a point to stay away from the police lines. Going to jail was not an effective way to make a statement; I had a louder voice outside, I reasoned. Yet here I was, security guard on my left, ushered back into the store where the cashiers and customers glared at me as if I were a convict. Hey! It's only a dollar's worth of cheese, my mind screamed. I stayed mum.

We went through thick closed doors to the upstairs. Who knew that the giant ceiling raised over the grocery section was lined around the perimeter with a second floor of offices? More significantly a detective sat up here with full view of the shoppers below. My bright colors would have targeted me first; my furtive glance served to confirm my guilt. As Bob Dylan so sagely put it "Those who live outside the law must be honest."

My security guard escort led me into a Safeway executive office where I protested that it was only a small chunk of cheese, please don't arrest me. Regaining a bit of composure in front of this suited man behind a desk, the very embodiment of my private war on the establishment, I went on to rail against Safeway's profits.

He also sat up straighter. "Safeway's profit margin is just 4%." He responded frostily. I didn't have time to doubt these figures because a policeman in full uniform – I checked the badge pinned to his chest – was now at the door and I was on my way out. He took the cheese as evidence.

In the police car, I realized I had a bigger problem: I was holding a joint of Mexican weed for Paul in my purse. Looking straight forward, I unzipped my purse and felt inside to locate the joint. I'd forgotten there were two joints, caught loosely in the leather crease at the bottom of my bag, the part filled with lint and old receipts. I panicked. Marijuana possession was a full-fledged crime. Damn! My mind swung into that crystal-clear survival mode where I know that my every action has to be the right one. I small-talked my way to the police station, while pulverizing the joints into tiny bits within my purse.

Once inside the station, I entered a stark no-nonsense room with a single woman officer, very calm and matter of fact, graying hair contained back in a rubber band. She looked me over and immediately tagged me "hippie," one of those newcomers whose alternative reality didn't match hers. Her eyebrows drew close together. I'd never been arrested before, so the journalist in me was slightly interested in this process of moving from one room to the next in a series of exchanges that would finally lead to the iron door clanking that I heard down the hallway. She emptied my purse, made note of my wallet, a book, a half bottle of shampoo, some Kleenex. I pretended to breathe. She zipped the bag back up and put the whole lot into a plastic bag with my name on it. So far, so good. She hadn't looked inside to see the greenish leaves caught in the lint. I desperately made the one allowed phone call and luckily a housemate answered. "Call back, two different calls, and get me out on OR, own recognizance," I pleaded. The respondent didn't sound too pleased with having to spring a shoplifter.

Another officer led me to an intermediary room, slightly larger. A stench pushed down on me from the hallway beyond: diarrhea, farts, and tears. I was joined by a 40-year-old woman, hair tinted red, pale Irish skin, nice-looking in a has-been kind of way. She wrung her hands in her lap. They left us alone. "What happened?" I asked. It turned out she had robbed a bank without a getaway car. Her boyfriend had put her up to it. Worse, she had her address on a slip of paper in her pocket. When the police checked on her address, they'd find a framed photo of her boyfriend. She'd failed him. She seemed more worried about this than the potential of five years jail time in front of her.

A tiny sliver of window connected me to the outside world and I could see it was getting dark. My body recoiled and my stomach knotted as I considered spending the night in jail. Where was Paul? Where were my liberators? I accepted a glass of water and sat there. "Brita Ostrom?" a third officer inquired. "Your friends called in. You're out. Your court date for misdemeanor shoplifting is this Friday." I didn't look at the redhead still sitting there. I stopped briefly back in the first room to retrieve my possessions bag, still intact. I didn't open it. No tempting fate.

Darkness had fallen when I walked out the front doors of the station, free on my own recognizance, and met my student housemate who'd driven his VW bug down to meet me. What a prince. I said very little as we drove the few blocks back to the rooming house. It turned out he'd called in twice, using different names and different voices, to get me out. Even though he was studying at the Catholic University and thereby part of the Establishment, he'd come through.

I fell into my slim bed, shaky and anxious about the day and also wondering where Paul was. After a fitful night's sleep and a morning cup of hot water with a tea bag submerged in it, Paul appeared. "Look what I made for you!" he pronounced. He unrolled a poster with a woman drawn cartoon style front and center, hands on her hips and mouth open wide. The slogan read "Mother speaks tonight on what is right!" He positioned it on my wall with thumbtacks. I didn't ask where he'd been. I suspected he'd crawled in with one of my friends and I didn't want to ask for details. I left the poster up for months, trying to fathom what to make of it.

I mulled over the Safeway escapade and my jailhouse visit. Paul had spotted the guard as we walked out of the store and moved to extract himself. Fair enough. I'd been shoplifting little things since my first accidental success at Bloomingdales. I hadn't paid for any of my lingerie in a year. I rationalized my stealing with my anti-capitalism stance. I choose poverty. Truth, I enjoyed this small triumph of getting something for free, though I'd never rob from an individual. I'd gotten away with it. I felt my half smile of triumph. I wasn't just a straight chick. I was waging war with the establishment and its wealth with every lacy item I lifted.

Now I was caught, and my day at the courthouse would give me a record. My utopian philosophy chaffed against today's morals where stealing from a supermarket was clearly wrong, even if that same supermarket might be deemed irresponsible to the hungry masses. I stood up, walked around, letting the events settle until I could see my mishap without so much push back. I had to give in and play it straight, accept ownership as a valid concept. This conclusion didn't sit well with me, yet I could see no other option.

As my defenses dropped, I felt the sting of shame. I was a thief, or a shoplifter at the very least. My face grew hot and my skin felt tight all over. This feeling wasn't what I was looking for in my new life. I paid attention. I never shoplifted again. It would be years before I told anyone. My parents and my brothers couldn't know. They still don't. I had failed to see the irony of my fancy underwear choices, only robbing for myself, high-end stuff I liked. It wasn't really about the industrial military complex. It was about me. In my defense, the following year Abbie Hoffman would extort us to "*Steal this Book*" as a means toward political action.

Friday morning, I pulled my hair back and smoothed on a skirt for my brief court appearance. Gotta look good. I met with a public defender who spent less than one minute interviewing me. When my name was called, I came nervously to the front as the charges were read out. Or rather: charge. Shoplifting cheese. The judge swung his gavel and pronounced, "Guilty, time served, no fine." I walked free. When I tried to expunge it later, the clerk found no record at all.

Back at our room, I let down my hair and pulled on my jeans with the flowery trim I'd sewn on the bottom, slipping my dark jacket over my skinny tee shirt. Paul trimmed his beard and hoisted the duffel over his shoulder, neat and tidy. No need to attract any more attention. We didn't talk. We took a Muni bus out to the Great highway and stuck out our thumbs, heading to our tree home one hundred and fifty miles South on the edge of the mountains, a getaway where reality lived somewhere else.

Tent raising

We were building our own home on the treehouse decking. Did this signal we were in a real relationship now, one that I could wrap my dreams around? This seemed like a couples' thing to do, create our nest. We are more than just travel companions, I reasoned over my last sip of coffee. We share a home. I left out the part about no walls. Leaving Esalen this afternoon, I gathered up two of the abandoned boards we'd stashed earlier. The contractor told us we could take whatever we wanted in the scrap pile. We wanted it all. The only catch: we had to carry every piece the mile-long 500-foot rise in elevation back to our camp site. Heavy! Meaning, a serious commitment and meaning a lot of weight for my shoulders. Today I snatched up two six-foot long 2x4s. Paul gathered up two 8-foot beams. These would create the frame for our plastic sheeting house. He gathered up a few lighter 2x2 pieces, too. I pocketed a few nails I spotted in the dirt. You never know.

"Did you ever do carpentry?" I asked him as we trudged around the first hairpin turn on the rutted road heading home.

"Sure," he grinned with a near wink that made me doubt it. Paul didn't categorize tasks as "art," "acting," "writing," although he was proficient in all of them. Instead, he lived every moment in full creative process. "Building" fit right in. Last week's first rain brought forth a panorama of new growth on our hillside. Paul stopped me and pointed to the sprouts springing forth out of cracks in the rocks. "God's paintbrush," he declared. We walked on and dropped off part of our load at the next turnout. Far enough for today, no need to overwork ourselves. We stepped more lightly up the mountain to our homemade dinner of yesterday's rice fried in olive oil with a few wild greens. I'd carefully scissored the thorns off thistle leaves and found them rather like spinach. Foraging became an art form, converting this weed to that food, this cast-off

Tent raising

wood to tomorrow's house, this torn shirt recycled as lashings to bind the house together. Exhausted now, I welcomed our small bonfire and Paul's tall tale about the horse that bucked him off and how he trained it for the Rose Bowl parade. I awaited the shared heat of our platform bed. A shooting star arched across the heavens.

"They're getting ready," said Paul, gazing skyward. He was waiting for the flying saucer to land. I wasn't. I dozed off. His imagination roamed way beyond my comfort zone sometimes.

Paul gathered the remaining boards in the morning and we set to work. Although my maternal Grandparents built their own home and raised all their food just two generations back, I stood idle while Paul arranged the boards in a semblance of a house. It would be six by eight feet, doorway in the front, a slant roof to slope off the rain. We needed a few more boards, I could see. This didn't slow Paul. He started by lashing the floor frame together. The first knot puzzled him and he re-arranged the boards and the lashing multiple times. He invented a new knot. Satisfied, he stood back and surveyed his work. I agreed; the multi-colored lashings were going to look good — if they held. I spotted a flaw, and complained, "I don't want to step over that board to get in." He looked at his layout, looked up at me, and re-arranged the front frame.

"Give me a hand," He commanded. "We need two people for this job." One by one we attached an upright to each corner. This took a lot of lashing to hold them stable, so I tore multiple strips of an old India bedspread. Paul wrapped each corner lashing in one direction and then reversed and wrapped it the other direction and up the board. Soon all four corners stood upright. Luckily the boards were already cut, predetermining the size. Before anything collapsed, Paul balanced a final beam across the top of one side, lashed it to the adjacent boards, and then lashed one end to the tree. He repeated this process three more times. I stood back, beaming with admiration at our home going up right before my eyes. He was using the two by twos for the top bracing because they were lighter, I could see. For good measure, he pounded the frame together where he could. We didn't have a hammer, so after a moment's thought, he pounded the nails using a shallow stone. He stood back, walked around it, looked at me, "Hey baby. We got ourselves a wigwam."

Wrapping the plastic sheeting around this structure took four hands and an occasional foot. We used a few smaller nails to secure it to the frame. The sheeting was one of the few things we purchased new. Called by its brand name, Visqueen, it was slightly thicker and therefore, we reasoned, more durable. We didn't want leaks. This thickness – 10 mm – added the surprise feature of almost transparent clarity. The canyon behind us, the bay tree overhead, the mountain on the east side all entered our bedroom and located us in wonderland. A single leaf fell onto our roof, completing our five-dimensional view. "I'll finish the door later," Paul promised himself. For the next season it was simply a loose flap of plastic with a light timber attached to the bottom so we could swing it in and out. Two bent nails hooked together secured it shut.

We immediately moved our bedding inside, relegated the duffle bags to the corner, added a rug next to the bed and our home was complete. I stepped through the flap-style door and could stand upright near the north end of the room. The room! We had done it. Paul lifted me up and swung me around in celebration.

The I-can-do-this attitude permeated every part of our existence. Not once did we visit the trendy new Whole Earth Catalog camping stores. We fashioned our lamps, cook stove, cook ware, utensils, wash tub and even our fire pit out of repurposed castaways. In this way we matched our Big Sur neighbors. When their car stopped running, the driver swore, got out, opened the hood, shook this and re-plugged that, added a spare piece of wire between two loose ends, and it was good to go. The anxious-looking passenger smiled in appreciation and their love was sealed.

The pregnant woman I had seen floating across the lawn on my arrival turned out to be named Storm, one of the founders of Esalen Massage and a local weaver. I slowly recovered from my shock at the news that she was planning to deliver this baby at home with the help of her husband and another friend who had just had a baby. "It's the most natural thing in the world," she explained to a very skeptical me. Storm's ease informed the local birthing coach in Monterey, who worked with her notions of multiple women attending the birth and sometimes singing to hasten the progress along. Storm and Ron's baby boy, River, bounced into his parents' arms healthy and joyous according to all reports. The news buzzed up and down the coast from dented truck to parked car at the post office. I listened, but I wasn't convinced. The medical model still laid claim to my reasoning.

Death was similarly addressed head on. When the neighbor's father died, he called the coroner, and then simply took Dad's body and buried him back in the canyon, The county intervened and reminded the neighbor that there were laws about things like that. With this not subtle prompt, he exhumed Dad and drove him to the funeral home for the prescribed legal rites. Then he retrieved him and the father returned, properly cremated, and was interred in the same canyon. But why not just bury him? I questioned.

Ensconced now in our mountain abode, we had an occasional visitor, mostly people Paul got stoned with, or an occasional notable such as John Lilly and his partner, intent on finding out how locals lived. Locals. That was us.

On this particular night, my old college friend Katie came visiting from New York City. We were just winding down for the evening, telling tales about the updated women's movement—"don't call her a chick!" Kate admonished me—and relishing each other's company. I saw a figure outside just as I was taking off my shoes. "Hey," I called out. I acted out of my New York City street-smarts protocol: always address unknown situations first, and loudly.

"Hey," a male voice called back. "It's Chris." Chris? Where was his truck? I was about to point out that it was too late to visit when he implored, "Look at me." I found the flashlight and opened the door to look at him: Tired, shoulders slumped, with dried blood across his face and around his eye. One eye was swollen shut. This looked bad. I ran through my checklist: no phone, late at night, no other help but me. I fainted at the sight of blood. I put that on the back burner. It was up to me.

Steeped

"C'mon in. Oh my." I tried not to blanch at all that blood smeared on his hands, too. I poured our warm water left from dinner tea into a bowl and found a clean cloth. "Sit down," I said sympathetically, clearing a space on the bed, our only remaining seat. Chris sat down quickly, obviously exhausted. I slowly wiped the blood from his face. Most of it had run from a single deep cut by his eye. He'd been lucky.

"My truck rolled over," he explained without my asking. "I carefully climbed out the door without jiggling it and walked here." One mile, and then this hill, with all these wounds. The eye incision was particularly grisly and a quarter-inch deep. It started bleeding again. I didn't want to thread a needle, but I didn't see anything else to do."

"Have a drink of this," I handed him a glass of cheap brandy I'd stashed. Maybe I should have some, too, to calm my anxiety. I'd never sewn anyone up before. I stood over him and poured a little brandy on the oozing wound. Alcohol disinfects, I reasoned. Ouch! I caught the first stitch, one side of the wound, and plunged the needle to the other side. I pulled the thread. He winced but stayed put. Stitch two, stitch three. It took three stiches to seal him back up completely. Katie didn't say a word. Neither did I. I'd just stitched a man up. Paul strolled in and proclaimed the work "adequate, very adequate." Now I had a glass of that brandy.

Just as a body builder slowly adds muscle from daily workouts at the gym, I added survival muscle and found it thrilling. I couldn't doctor - I was too squeamish - but I could commune with the medical world, speak up for myself. If I could stitch a man up — leaving almost no scar —what else could I take on? I stood up straight, almost proud.

Winter in Big Sur

The Giant Sycamores shed their golden plate-sized leaves revealing skeletal branches that now arched over Route One where it traversed the Big Sur Valley. I spotted an early monarch butterfly dropping out of a Eucalyptus tree. "They're here!" Lorna exclaimed, as if witnessing a wingéd oracle. Just as winter pulled into view, Esalen Institute had a fall of its own making. I received a phone call from the front office as I was packing my duffle in San Francisco to head back to the mountain. "Don't come. We don't need you for that short-term job we talked about." OK. I wasn't really counting on this gig. But her next sentence set the world spinning backward. "We're letting everyone go. We're paring the staff down to twelve."

I struggled to sort it out. No job? Ok. It was a short-term gig I'd been hired for, cleaning Virginia Satir's cabin. An acclaimed social thinker, she must be leaving, too, I mused. Slowly the magnitude sank in. I'd hitched to Big Sur with Esalen as my target, although the actual bull's eye turned out to be the tangential community. Still, the Institute was a hot bed of study and experiments about human potential, spring-loaded with Aldous Huxley's work, Abe Maslow's seminal findings on self-actualizing, and the current social unrest in America. It couldn't just sink! This was awful. Also, I couldn't reach Paul to gauge his reactions.

I paused to take this in. "What about the gate guards? What about the kitchen?" I responded faintly.

"It's winter, not much traffic. Those left will staff the gate as well as do everything else." Paul had just been rehired back at the gate; now he was laid off again. A whole new box of questions opened: Would he stay on in his caretaking gig? Would I now be paying for our food? And what about Esalen itself? What was behind all this?

I hung up the phone, threw on my jacket, and strode outside into the San Francisco breeze. I kept walking, careful to avoid the steep uphill route back to the Haight. I tried to stay level-headed. The future that I normally didn't give much thought now loomed cloudy.

What had happened? Over several days, other frantic phone calls, and a surprise visit from a former staffer now on the loose and checking out the San Francisco scene, a story took shape. Bud Leighton, the general manager who 86-ed Paul and me, the same guy who had just moved an attractive wife into his trailer, had also done a poor job keeping the books. Suddenly, unannounced, the money was gone. Embezzled? No real proof. Just gone. Badly managed? No doubt. The whole operation was sinking out of control. The residential program—twenty students enrolled for a winter of intense learning with noted group psychologist Will Schutz—was still in full swing. Now, part of their experience at Esalen would include taking over day-to-day management, staffing the front desk, serving meals to the few short-term guests, and yes, sitting at the gate shack, along with the handful of remaining staff.

A few days later I caught a ride back to Sur and made the mountainous hike in the daylight. I rounded the final bend to the back side of the hill and hollered forth, announcing my arrival. Paul buoyantly emerged from the woods, stepping lightly over fallen limbs toward me. He opened his arms wide, invitingly. "Hey baby, love ya!" A big hug, like nothing had changed. His body felt warm, sweaty. We sat down by the unlit fire pit. He pulled out his loose Bugler tobacco and rolled a cigarette while stretching out his legs, then bending forward to retie his leather boots. He lit up his rolled tobacco. The high cross-canyon vista of rolling hills shone green after the early rains, reminding us that we were surrounded by beauty. Did it matter about money? I struggled to voice the concerns that had rapped loud in my head all week.

"Paul, the gig at Esalen is gone." I paused, not knowing where to go next. I took a deep breath and plunged into the unknown territory. "What are your plans?"

"Hey baby, we're free! Somebody gave me a bag of rice and I bought some bacon at the Village store, so we've got dinner. Did you bring carrots? You want to hike back and see how I fixed the water source? I found a bigger tin can for the catchment." He twinkled his blue eyes at me, smiled, and rose in one easy gesture. I took this in, laughed, and my doubts dissolved, delighted in this moment with Paul, our clean fresh water from a stream above, and an open horizon. I recalled the verse from my childhood Sunday School, "Consider the Lilies of the field, they toil not yet even Solomon in all his glory was not arrayed like one of these." Maybe I worried too much. Maybe I could just trust, as he did. The San Francisco diggers, his old friends, said, "Today is the first day of the rest of your life," and believed in all things free. Did I dare give this a try?

"Wait a minute." I stashed my backpack securely in the plastic tent on the tree platform, changed into my worn leather shoes, and picked up my pace, trying to keep up with him. This hillside was our home. I stayed a week.

On my return ride headed toward the city, the driver pulled into the Coast Gallery Parking Lot. "I'll be heading North in a bit, if you want to wait," the driver assured me. OK. I'll check it out.

I didn't see Lucille. She ran the Gallery. An old timer in every way, her late day gatherings featuring notable characters such as Alan Watts were favored among the locals. Today, my attention was drawn to the clothes lining the back wall. In vivid patterns and stretchy prints, I recognized them as the garb worn by SF Rock stars who strutted and swayed on stage. Jeannie Rose had a wait list for her designs, and here they were, ready to wear. Big Sur never failed to surprise. I'd hoped to sew similar garments, but I didn't know where to begin. I held up the mirror to a snugly fitted pant suit, a scoop-necked sleeveless model with deeply belled bottoms in cool paisley swirls. All this hiking had trimmed my body and I hadn't noticed my new curves. "Try it on," urged the sales attendant. I slipped off my everyday jeans and plain pullover knit shirt and slid into this new shape. The fabric was like extra skin, moving with me. Looking in the mirror, I beheld a new Brita. More than that, a new character. Could I take this on? I stood out brightly, as if I wanted to be noticed, to excite the viewer. I tried on the nearby bead-fringed shawl and entered a mythic realm. The sales attendant laughed as I danced around the store.

"I'll save up for this one," I sang. I'd never worn actual costumes before, but why not? Somehow Esalen's demise and Paul's free spirit propped open my imagination. Lifting myself out of the spell, I put back on my old attire, but now I rolled back my shoulders, tilted my head, and I knew that I could be anyone I wanted to be. I caught up with the driver, and off we sped, back to the big city.

My new schedule became standard: one week in Big Sur; ten days in the city. I worked temporary jobs, in offices and department stores. I purchased apple juice and lightweight staples and fixed a peanut butter sandwich for today's journey. Last winter, I'd been safely tucked into my marriage and my Haight Street apartment with the big back yard. I hadn't really noticed weather except for the months of fog. So, this morning when I headed out to the King's Highway, thumb stretched toward Big Sur, I failed to notice the voluminous dark gray clouds emerging from the Southeastern sky.

The first ride came easily, lifting me all the way to Castroville. However, this turnoff had proved a tough place to hitch in the past and today was no exception. Finally, a pouty couple picked me up and drove me, wordless, to four corners in Monterey, so nicknamed for the gas station on each corner, a jumping-off place. Here I left the route to Monterey and stayed on Route One southbound. It could take me another hour and a half to get to Hot Springs Canyon.

By now rain was starting to fall, so I ducked into Denny's and grabbed a hot soup to go. Back on the street, it was already getting dark. I could hear the high-pitched bark of the sea lions at the wharf. Somehow, they never sounded happy. I had to get a ride soon! This army surplus camo raincoat kept my top half dry, but my jeans were already speckled with droplets. These shoes weren't waterproof. A beat-up ford truck with a young lanky woman at the wheel swerved over, hailed me into the cab and briskly headed south. "I'm skipping the hardware store stop," she muttered. "This storm's coming." She gave me a serious look. As we drove south, I felt the wind increase. The truck seemed to move sideways on its own accord as we hit the Point Sur lighthouse straight-away. By now she had the windshield wipers on full speed, banging away.

She was bound for Gorda further South, to her old man and their caretaker cabin. "Are you sure?" She asked with a worried look when I indicated my stop and struggled to get out of the truck and into the night. The wind hit me and I pulled my backpack tighter to my body.

" I'll be fine. I grew up in Seattle so what's a little rain!" I joked. She laughed and drove off. I fished out my flashlight. It glowed dimly. After I climbed over the chain-link gate and squished through the mucky roadbed for another two hundred feet, it gave out altogether. So much for the promised nine lives of Eveready batteries. Paul and I had practiced walking in the dark, hoping to develop our other senses, so this would be a good test. I wish I knew if Paul had gotten the message that I was coming today. I took a deep sigh and re-adjusted my pack, now soggy.

Was it my imagination or was the rain actually falling harder? I could hear the rivulets of water race through the small driveway gullies on my left. Something rolled down the hillside and plopped onto the roadbed behind me. On my right was the canyon, a fall of several hundred feet. The uphill climb coupled with the downward pull of my heavier pack fought against my speed. I knew that after I crossed the western face of the hillside, I would turn almost 90° to start the canyon wall traverse. But where was that turn?

Now I couldn't see anything and at this elevation, the wind blew harder, from the South. At the mouth of the canyon, it seemed to aim straight for me, hitting me in the face and blowing off my hood. Wet! I struggled to get my bearings, mindful of the canyon drop. My strides grew shorter, more tentative. All my senses opened wide. I didn't even have time to worry. I focused on each soggy step.

Finally, the sound changed, and I could hear the creek echoing directly in front of me and then beside me. I'd made it round the bend. The wind whipped through the redwoods below. Another few hundred yards, and I was at our home base ledge. No lights greeted me. "Hey!" I sang out hopefully. My voice disappeared into the noisy night. But inside the tent, a light flickered and then glowed steadily. He was home. I was safe for now and welcomed.

I carefully opened the tent flap, holding firm to keep the wind from blowing it out of my hands. I set down my wet pack, hung my dripping raincoat on a nail, and left my wet clothes in a heap on the floor. My hands shook as I took a big gulp of water from the jug. Paul barely rolled over in bed. His sleepy "Hi baby" never sounded better. The platform rocked on its tree limb foundation and leaves plastered the wet roof.

In the morning, we awoke as the sun appeared over the hilltop. Warmth! I could hang up my clothes, open the tent, and we'd be dry in no time. "In Big Sur we're all wash and wear," ran the local lore. Two more months of winter awaited us. I could tell that timing was everything, and "A day at a time" meant really paying attention to the here and now and the rainclouds overhead. A tent through the Big Sur winter? Why not?

Leaving to Arrive: The Long Walk

Paul was Irish to the core. Not only was he an O'Rourke, but he loved to play with the English language in poetry and lampoon, enjoyed a taste for alcohol, waxed gallant around the female species, and knew how to contact the spirits when he needed to. "Have you heard, *'May the Road rise up to meet you?'*" I smiled inquiringly, asking after the old Irish blessing encompassing the universal elements of earth, air, fire and water. *May the road rise up to meet you. May the wind be always at your back. May the sun shine warm upon your face; the rains fall soft upon your fields...*

He answered in the negative and kept on walking. Yet in Big Sur the road really did rise up to meet us. Each uphill step found a new foot bed, a new angle on the earth. We weren't just tromping; this land was meeting us. Today Paul was back to wearing his old white sneakers, soles so worn that they molded readily to each bump in the road like a moccasin.

We set out hiking to an open-air New Year's party at a nearby construction site, Burns Creek. "Hey, c'mon by tonight. Some good drumming," was how the invitation arrived, with a wink. We walked down the rutted driveway past the half-built house. I recognized the drummers gathered in the shadows. We'd hung with one of the carpenters who now loaded up the fire with the slash left over from their day's work. Even though it was midwinter, the balmy night air warmed me in my handwoven wool shawl flung over my shoulders. A slight wind stirred the leaves. I craned my neck upward to take in the brilliant Milky Way splashed across the mid-sky. The mentholated scent of the eucalyptus leaves sweetened the campfire. The surroundings altered my senses on this night, the closeout of 1967. I smiled at Paul.

Near the fire a blonde man with hair pulled into a neat ponytail played a plaintive song on his end-blowing bamboo flute. Darn! I wish I'd brought my flute to join in. The drums sat idle, drumheads turned toward the fire to warm them up and draw out the ambient moisture. But the other instruments also sat idle: a silver flute lay on a chair and a guitar was still in its case. A half empty Coors beer bottle sat on a stump. A girl lay sleeping in the bed of a pickup truck with its back gate open.

Taking it all in, "Funny," I concluded, puzzled. I'd expected more of a party vibe. A dark-haired man with a trimmed beard gave us a high five but kept on course toward a half-built structure in the shadows. I began to feel ill at ease. I lifted my hair from the back of my neck and I counseled myself that I just wasn't used to parties at construction sites. These were locals we bumped into regularly at various jobs or at the post office. I'd seen one of the guys working at Esalen, rebuilding the counter in the office. I didn't know them. Paul recognized Billy from his stint on the gate. "Hey" he called out. No response came back.

We spotted several of the musicians and a few hangers-on under the rafters of the half-built house. Paul moved to join them, but the circle tightened as he approached. The flute player stood up, glanced our way and commented under his breath, "No fun here. Bunch a' smack's come in." Heroin again.

Paul strolled back. I stood up. "Let's go," he said tersely, already in motion toward the upward incline of the driveway. I followed his lead instantly. I couldn't put my finger on the undercurrent, at once unwelcoming, dark, and yet communal. We were outsiders. Scoring hard drugs and then using them with reckless abandon was a kind of proving ground in Sur. I could hear the low talk and drawn out breath, the nearly-friendly slaps on the back. They had to trust each other. A false move or a doctored fix could land you in jail or dead. Each knew that it could easily be his friend who did him in. I understood now the high barriers for acceptance by these locals who tackled the hills, lived in rough shacks, fought over women, worked hard and forgot about the world they left behind as best they could. "Horse," as they called it, would be their forgetful friend tonight. Yes, we were outsiders to this lifestyle.

Hitting the uphill Route One never felt so good. We had a new year in front of us. By leaving the party we dodged a rough evening of undertone newcomer insults. We paused before crossing the next bridge. "Heavy!" was all Paul said into the darkness. The moon had already set, but the starlight reflected on the road, illuminating our way. I could easily see Paul's forward moving body striding ahead of me, his short wavy hair catching the wind. We picked up our pace. Our mood followed suit. At this hour we could walk right down the middle of the highway without worrying about an unexpected car. The few travelers still moving tonight were easily visible from a long way off. It was just us. Paul turned and smiled at me, kicking up his heels in a small jig. I responded with my arms-outstretched in a slow spin. This was our world, this night spangled with a million stars.

We walked. We weren't going anywhere special. The very act of walking had taken on its own meaning. Originally, I walked this road to get somewhere. Then I walked to return to the land, to meet the ancestors. It fit with my survivor philosophy. When we walked tonight, one mile, then two, I felt the old year's dilemmas — my cut-short marriage, my indecision about career, my grief over the wasted war — all fall away. This walking through a starlit night cleaned me, brought me to my skeletal bare bones. This was me, quite simply just walking. A few more steps and I caught the edge of the pavement, giving my ankle a slight twist, just enough to provoke a limp for the next quarter mile. This pain called me to be present, to pay attention to each footfall. The walk took on a spiritual dimension, uniting me with all those who walked before in religious rites, in temples in Egypt, the Camino in Spain, the walkabout in Australia. Looking upward, I felt a similar kinship with shepherds who had looked to the stars for their direction as they kept watch over their flock.

Paul set a good pace, lengthening his stride, silencing his usual song. We became one with the night, two sojourners walking the planet. We weren't alone in our walking. While we didn't meet a soul, up and down the coast young people like us were walking along this 75-mile stretch of coastline called Big Sur. For a local, it was nothing to walk five miles back home after visiting a friend. The Sur was a land of walkers. No one commented on it. Walking came as naturally as rain and fog. When we came down with the flu, we walked it off, Big Sur's medicine. We all knew the freedom of the open road, the opportunity to go North or South, to trust in the earth. Big Sur walkers experienced the loose wrap of beauty around them, be it stars or sea or redwoods, or the symphony of the creeks. This land was best experienced walking. And that is exactly what we did. I listened to our footfalls in the night and dreamed a wide-open world.

"Hey honey" Paul hailed me. "Look at this." Paul never said "Let's rest." He wasn't one to ease up. Yet stopping like this was part of him, to breath in our surround. We burrowed onto a stony mound of dirt sprouting new grasses and fixed our gaze seaward. Paul reached in his shirt pocket and pulled out a tightly rolled skinny joint. He extracted a book of matches from his other pocket and lit it up. "Happy New Year," he said softly in my ear and smiled at me, then coughed as he exhaled. This Michoacán weed was rough, cured with lots of leaf intact. Yet the coughing seemed a part of it, that intake of breath triggering a brighter wilder world. I inhaled carefully, slowly. At the last minute I too erupted into a cough spasm. We laughed. "Far in!" His voice spun out as we watched constellations drop into the sea. He scanned the sky for his dreamed-of flying saucers. Seeing none, he hugged me tighter and his hands on my body reminded me that he was a man and I was his woman.

Too soon, the first light of dawn brightened the eastern sky, bringing the west face of the Santa Lucia range into sharper dark contrast. Now the edges of the rocky cairns and boulders stood out, sentinels watching us from ancient times. We solemnly acknowledged this hook-up with the Ancient Ones as we gazed skyward from this mound of dirt carelessly left by a bulldozer operator. "Happy 1968." I bit his earlobe in reply. Paul always knew he had all the time in the world. I knew we had today, and that was enough.

Unmapped Departure

Difficult as it was to get to Big Sur on its singular windy road, skirting past fallen rock and the occasional broken-down car, it was even harder for me to stay put once I arrived. With Paul I felt an ease, at home, yet the plastic-sheeted basecamp, packed knapsack, and lack of refrigeration for food storage spelled temporary in a way I couldn't mistake. Paul lovingly referred to me as his travel companion and I never introduced him as my old man. He wasn't. He was my sprite and my travel guide and he was also occasionally crazier than a loon when he got going, arms flapping as he welcomed flying saucers or cried out at the establishment for Hollywood misdeeds. Remember, he was an actor by trade.

I, on the other hand, was mindful of my dwindling back account – it had dipped below my $300 minimum –my Enovid birth control prescription, my dental check-up, and my one room flat in San Francisco. The winter rains chilled even our outdoor fire site, so last week I headed north to the City and worked for Kelly Girls Office Temps, typing briefs in the back room of an aged lawyer's office in an aged building on Market Street. "This has to be the most boring job ever," I fumed to myself in the late afternoon as the daylight faded through the high windows facing the traffic on Market Street three stories below. Thank God for the last page, a paycheck to keep me going two more weeks.

Now I was back in Sur, hiking up the mountain with a backpack of fresh food in just enough light to keep from bouncing into rocks.

I sensed a change even before I made it round the last turn. Maybe it's the wind pushing upward off the ocean, I told myself. When our translucent home came into view, no lantern light shown forth. Odd. My pulse quickened as I considered the possibilities: he's dead somewhere. He got a job. Finally, I hit the most dreaded possibility: he left. In fact, his knapsack, while still in its customary spot, had folds in its canvas, indicating some of the contents had been removed. And his backpack – I quickly took inventory – was missing. Ok. Maybe he hitched to town and was spending the night. My jaw clenched. I always worried about other women, though only one or two had caught his eye. I spread cheese on crackers, opened the apple juice and poured a glass. I squatted down in the tent and made myself comfortable after the day's journey and now this unsettling surprise.

The night's quiet crashed into my head, the aloneness of this place beneath a mountain and above a canyon, ledge living. Our tree platform was in the shadows of one of those hilly earth folds you see out an airplane window. I heard the wind rustle oak leaves far across the canyon, then slowly circle toward me. Now my bay tree was a-flutter, breezy enough to rattle the one loose piece of plastic sheeting on the back corner. I listened more carefully, alert, aware that my ears were my best defense again this black night a mile from anyone. A coyote let loose a barking fit on the south canyon face. She called again and this time a yipping arose behind me, to the north. Each coyote took a different note, then paused so the lead song dog could respond. Back and forth, they told a story or sang of perils.

No signs of civilization lay between these coyotes' nightly cavorting and the Salinas Valley 20 miles eastward, just wild land and a few cattle, maybe a feral horse. When Paul was here, he'd howl back; he filled the space in a way that I didn't. I sensed the void, the emptiness, the snap of small twigs. My ears started ringing. I was still thirsty, so I carefully made my way across the gangplank from the tree platform to the solid ground. If I fell now…ok, another thought I didn't want to address. I can do this. I filled my cup with water and, resisting the impulse to crawl, strode back across the plank to my tent and into bed. Our bed. This was my choice, after all, and I was certainly safer than I had been in New York City. Or so I told myself.

I lay in the plastic tent and contemplated the clear roof overhead with its pattern of scattered leaves, hoping to find an answer there. Paul was gone. Sure, he'd come back — his duffle lay undisturbed in the corner — but for me, maybe the jig was up. Paul

Steeped

excelled in dropping out—or dropping in, as he preferred to say. I too railed against the establishment with its focus on materialism and this Viet Nam war that it created. Haight had taught me to "put free in front of any word," according to the Diggers. I'd picked up today's shirt at the free store on Haight. But I didn't go this far, to just drop my partner with no backward glance. Based on my recently witnessed San Francisco commune food fight over stale refrigerated apples, I'd grown to doubt the hippie edict of "peace, not power".

Paul and I acted like lovers; we defined our relationship as travel companions, free, uncommitted. Yet jealousy easily raised its nasty head resulting in a hasty slap of the palm across my cheek, permitted in this counterculture where expression trumped manners. "Ouch!" A few hours apart and we were back in the saddle. Paul's poetic self sometimes spoke his love, his passion. I didn't have those words to reply, and in fact I didn't talk much. We'd met a year ago and hitched many miles together. I was in awe of his unencumbered lifestyle. When I first struck up a conversation with Paul in a Haight Street coffee shop, He told me he slept in Golden Gate Park. He carried no baggage and no money either, but his blue eyes sparkled and a smile peeked out beneath his unkempt beard. His energetic walk and easy chuckle contrasted with my soon-to-be former husband's disbelief in everything. Sometimes Paul intently looked right into my eyes while he held my hand softy, captivated me. In those moments, I forgot he was an actor. I agreed with him about a lot of things that I hadn't really articulated, about spirit and the need to free up energy in the body, to really express myself fully in a meaningful way. Later Paul would send an illustrated letter to me without a return address, speaking "I love Brita now;" speaking of freedom; "I want to get free to create a house, love, and a sense of caring, a happy gypsy with rooms that go right up to the sky." That letter would arrive much later.

Today, his charm had grown cold. I sat on the log and looked out up at clouds spilling over the hills to the east. the My eyes caught a large bird, a vulture, flying motionless in the canyon updraft. Once he was overhead, he took off to the south. Taking in the breadth of sky and depth of the canyon walls, I sat back on my log perch and let this moment roll over me. My vision expanded and my brain felt wider. I sensed my affinity with the rocks and the trees. I'd changed over the past year, become more settled in myself. As for Paul, I realized that his arm-waving riffs influenced a few of his listeners to really look at the narrow range of their lives, but just as often he turned people off. Too much! The irony of his so-called freedom from work and my income gleaned from temporary typing jobs in the slick San Francisco Pyramid building or grimy South of Market settings wasn't lost on me either. I agreed, it was my choice to work rather than forage. I didn't trust *the flow* as he did; I didn't imagine that food would arrive, or a ride would always take us where we wanted to go. Was I uptight to be concerned about the next meal, to want a choice in what I ate or where I would lay my head?

Every other week I stuffed small brown paper bags of rice, oats, raisins, butter, and cashews, a carton of eggs, and a pound of ground beef into my pack as I exited the city for our tent on the mountain. Paul and my Rutgers collegemate-come-west, Bob Leoniwicz nicknamed CZ, grinned and expressed almost reverent appreciation when I arrived breathless after ascending the hill with the extra weight. CZ always showed up for my arrival from his camp down the hill. My provisions bought them pan-fried hamburgers, time to hunker by the fire, pass the joint and breathe deeply, go with the flow. CZ entertained us singing his version of the newly invented Moog synthesizer or riffing one of his poems. I welcomed Paul's hug, the joy I brought them, and I felt loved in that moment. Yet I had bluffed one of the requirements for dropping out: I still worked. The word "enabling" hadn't been invented yet.

Paul's love of the vine changed my shopping list. I no longer tucked a bottle of wine into my pack for a romantic evening together, knowing it could fuel a shouting spree about the Man, anyone in authority, the ills of civilization. Once started, he'd empty every bottle, shaming any host who tried to keep one hidden. Soon his actor-trained voice would ring out, blasting movie producers and telling tales on Jimmy Stewart. He offered a loud invitation to everyone within hearing distance to open to the spirit, or to welcome the flying saucers. He looked skyward and signaled to a moving light overhead, invoking contact with extraterrestrials who would take him with them.

He ranted onward, yearning to expand human consciousness into directions I couldn't stretch. "We're born with knowing." He paused deeply and went on, "We just have to tap into it, get rid of what I learned in Art school." The world is wrong; goodness is smashed every moment. Dare to get rid of our book learning, drop fully in to each experience, drop out of any damn occupation or identity that define us. "Acid will change the culture, all our relationships," he challenged. He wasn't mean. He rode his own tirade and didn't notice when his audience quietly picked up and moved into the shadows. Then he'd look around the empty campfire circle and chuckle. An arm waving drunk, yes, but also an Irish drunk, righteous to the core with a gift of too many words all aimed at the evil of the establishment and its bind on our spirit. These images churned now in my mind.

A decade later he wrote reflectively, "I was afraid of the freedom to learn from people. I thought I'd find out how rotten and unfeeling I was, while pretending to be a friend. I wanted to be a valuable person to you and others. I started to see through my appearance of security as non security. Now I've gone without much of the beauty I pretended I didn't need." Perhaps he was thinking of these hills, and of me, when he penned that note. I shivered in the morning air.

A familiar holler interrupted my reverie. Who? Not Paul. It was my pal, CZ, up to share the morning fire and then hike to his gate guard gig down the hill. We'd been friends since Rutgers in New Jersey, and he followed me here, happy to find a home for his poetry and a way to earn a dollar. I stood up to greet him, still garbed in yesterday's clothes, gritty-eyed and grumpy.

"Where's Paul?" I asked as calmly as I could muster. I didn't want to let on how scared I was. Abandonment was not part of my repertoire. After all, we were just travel companions.

"He left last week, day after you left. I think he was going south," replied CZ, playing the same charade. He knew how important Paul was to me. "Drunk, with a bottle of hooch in his hand." He added.

"Oh," my short response. Paul had spent a decade in Hollywood as a stunt man, actor, illicit boyfriend, and street artist. He couldn't stand that city. So why return?

I stoked the fire and added coffee water to the blue enamel pot. I carefully placed it on the tippy grill balanced on stones over the flames. I added a bigger twig, blew on the fire, and then sat back for many minutes. When the water was nearly boiling I removed the pot, using my shirtsleeve as a potholder, and spooned in the coffee grounds. After they slowly settled to the bottom, I poured it slowly, carefully. I found my chipped enameled cup and a tin one for CZ and filled them with the steaming brew. Camp coffee. CZ and I sat silently, enjoying the fragrant dark beverage, careful of the hot metal rim. I dug an apple out of my backpack and cut it into a blackened pan of bubbling oatmeal. Once the coffee was finished, I spooned the cereal into our cups, added sunflower seeds and powdered milk. We made small talk about the day ahead. Really, all I could think about: What now?"

Soon CZ disappeared around the bend, off to work, no doubt glad to escape my gloom. I rinsed the dishes, set them to dry on the grass in the morning sun, and picked up my backpack. No sense sticking round. I found a piece of rough paper and wrote my friend Miki "As you know I was into a very heavy trip with a fellow I met in Haight but then split and went to Big Sur and I followed....now he split and I doubt if he will ever return because that's how he is, the mythic wanderer. He'll come into town, lay a beautiful new reality on you, and disappear, mysteriously, into the night. And somehow that's what I always expected him to do, because I must have asked him a thousand times to be sure to let me know if he decides to split. Now he's gone. Paul and I were into such a heavy thing and loved each other so terribly much and yet at the same time hassled each other so very much." I re-read it to make sure I hadn't left anything out, and noticed I'd whitewashed my pain. I wasn't ready to feel that part. I stuffed it into an outside pocket of my backpack to mail later.

I scribbled CZ a note, added a line for Paul, then sat down. Where should I go? My quandary devolved into anger. How could he! After all, I had a life to lead, I couldn't wait around. I'd been left behind, a travel companion to no one but myself. I wouldn't admit my fear of living on my own in this vast backwater of hot springs canyon, three gullies converging in a wide drop, and a rock face we called the White Cliffs of Dover setting an ominous white back wall. The canyon rang with creek song and the sway of redwoods, never silent, sometimes crashing. To the Southeast across the creek rose a small mountain, its granite face fringed with trees looking down at us. The peak caught the morning sun first and today it promised a fair day ahead. This untouched mountain rise and canyon drop sang to me the native American spiritual, "Beauty before me, beauty behind me."

Still, I sensed a darkness, too, a primordial sense of eminent danger or death or a bad smell. A psychic confirmed this. "I see a dark presence behind your home." The following years I personally witnessed a car rollover and the driver's miraculous uphill scramble. Then, a truck rollover and the unfortunate death of the itinerate black man called Three Feathers. Two decades later, our world was shaken to its core by a downward rolling boulder, smashing into the skull of Dick Price while hiking alone. These calamities occurred within shouting distance of our tree platform. Unwary hikers would scramble from the ridge top down the hillside, only to meet the slick 50-foot fall of solid white rock just above the Hot Springs Creek bed. We'd hear their frantic cries. We'd holler instructions to return upward and veer toward the North until they reached the edgy hot springs trail. We hoped they'd make it. Those who sought safety hiked elsewhere.

A Bend in Route One

I wanted out, out of this dream with a wild cowboy actor who left me without a note. However, Paul's departure flung me into a corner. I was here because I had wanted out last summer, out of the Haight's summer of love, out of mainstream thinking with its plaid sports jacket, maybe out of my marriage. So, if I left this mountain ledge, I'd be out again, far out, out on a limb, out without any anchor at all. Paul preferred to say, "far in," but that didn't apply in this case. I felt I was instead spinning outward, further away from my known center. Sure, I was smart and looked ok and now I knew I could survive more than I had imagined. But I wasn't willing to dive into the drift of life completely, to crash on strangers' floors and eat day-old bread with no care from whence my next penny came. To trust completely. No way. This was not the creativity I dreamed of. I needed flashlights and shoelaces and self-respect.

The dampness penetrated my log seat, chilling my buttocks. I rose and strolled away from the campsite to overlook the deep Hot Springs canyon as it split the hills and gushed downward into the Pacific. The winter rains flooded the creek, filling my ears with its roar. From this height, Esalen Institute appeared a tiny square of clearing and cars to the South. The splendid old Murphy house was nearly invisible in its cover of Cypress trees near the Pacific cliffside. Grey clouds hovered over the ocean, breaking up the blue line of the sea meeting the sky. I looked slowly left to right, taking in this broad horizontal curve of the earth that was all mine this morning. I breathed in my smallness – a speck, really – in this vast scape of land and time. Mammoth sharp rocks rose randomly in front of me, relics of an ice age glacier, watchful sentinels over the Big Sur coastline. Scrubby wild lilac trees and chaparral clung to the face of this unnamed hill. One dark cloud escaped and moved in my direction. More rain would fall soon.

I stood on the rocky narrow road feeling smug in my mastery of living at civilization's edge, without the too-soft comforts of a warm bed or three-course dinner. My Mother's love of the proper home with china didn't touch me here. I could let my wildness out, holler and sing out over the canyon, run full throttle down this hill. Yet now I stood still, uncertain.

The day grew warmer around me. Not waiting – hoping - for Paul to return meant I'd be alone. I'd sailed into this relationship while still marginally married. I proudly called myself a hippie. Still, I couldn't imagine myself without a man in my life, someone holding me and telling me I was beautiful. "I love you." To keep those words coming, I'd put a lot into this relationship, including dangerous hitchhike rides and dull work.

I pulled out that crumpled letter to Miki and added a note of honesty. "I keep peeking into a more spiritual understanding (I'm learning about Tarot cards and the I Ching). But until I get myself settled for a while at least with an old man who I really dig then here's where I'm at. Until I can really learn to do my own thing and make my own responses, I can't really be part of any lasting relationship." Could I step out of that paradox?

I stumbled and lost my footing on a loose rock, jarring me back to the here and now. What choice did I have? I wasn't the main caretaker here, and Paul was gone. Would leaving the mountain mean I was selling out on my commitment to higher levels of consciousness? To living with just basics, in raw nature? A little flicker of excitement rose in my chest. What next? Without Paul, I'd no longer be berated if I waited tables at the hot springs. Esalen Institute had weathered a serious financial downturn in November, nearly closing. The skeleton crew of paying residents plus a cook and a housekeeper kept the place running after the General Manager turned out to be a bum. Cash donations had apparently come through, and now they might need help in the remodeled kitchen for the anticipated spring surge.

Before the sun rose much higher, I was back on the highway, thumb pointing northward. I had an invite from a French

Steeped

Journalist in San Francisco to see the Cream at the Fillmore. .I didn't want to miss meeting Eric Clapton.

Ten days later and next trip South, I took a nudge from the spring blossoms around me and instead of walking up the hill to my mountain home, I rode on for another quarter mile and walked down the hot springs driveway. Last week the sign read "Big Sur Hot Springs," Now it was replaced with the much simpler "Esalen Institute," later to be capped with, "by reservation only."

I searched out the kitchen manager, Peter Melchior, and laid my case on the table: I wanted a job. "Sure," he said, "Start April 6." The day after my 24th birthday.

I bounced up the mountain, and this time, Paul was back. He stretched his arms wide, but his murmured, "Hey baby,' sounded muffled to my ears. He felt apart, different. For one thing, his new colorful clothes were all hand sewn. "Look!" he exclaimed, and he turned slowly and then broke into a stomping jig. He'd designed a pull-on cotton shirt with open collar and loose pants with matching patchwork. No more blue jeans. Good looking! He knew how to sew? "Just learned," he pronounced. He'd stopped at an ashram South of LA and fallen under the spell of a sewing machine. In fact, he had a whole bag of new garments, though nothing, I couldn't fail to note, for me. This story seemed disingenuous, but I took it in. Welcome back. He lit up a joint, something special from Michoacán, Mexico.

I told him about my job success. He was still on the outs with Esalen after that old pot smoking incident. They'd hired him back briefly, laid him off along with the rest of the staff, and more recently his stealth midnight bath trips had closed the door again. He harbored philosophical differences over its moneyed guests who only pretended to drop out. Esalen wasn't the enemy, but it was less than friendly territory. His response, "Way to go!" and smile looked made-up. Even though he wasn't outwardly possessive of me, Paul knew I'd find takers down at the hot springs. So, we had that difficult conversation. A soft parting of ways. I could always sleep at the foot of the mountain road in the little glen. Without a tear – it would take me time to rediscover my vulnerability – I walked away. He carried my bedroll, I carried my pack, and I decamped. I stumbled on the sharp turn going down, just as I had stumbled coming up, but now I wore sneakers and recovered more quickly. We stashed the stuff in the glen, fragrant with wild lilacs. He hugged me tight and whispered those sweet nothings that all actors learned on stage. I hugged his warm body, pulled away, turned, and stepped over the chain gate back to the highway, momentarily saddened.

    I pulled my hair off my face and tucked it behind my ear, glancing up to the clouds, inhaling. I was as sorry to leave my mountain home as I was to leave Paul and the love we shared. Later he summed it up, "Anyway, it was a home on a hill under a tree with you and your beautiful people. You gave me so much more than peanut butter." Later he added, "When I dismantled the tree house I felt finished, as though what had been was all lost and I was alone." I continued walking south to the hot springs. This quiet stretch of highway was familiar, too. As it turned out, I would be back up this hill within six months. The mountain and I had more to learn from each other.

Feeling Out Loud

I summed it all up for my friend Miki in a 1968 letter,

"Did I ever send you the letter saying I was moving down permanently (as permanently as I ever do anything!) to Big Sur... The most important reason being, as usual, an extremely heavy love affair with a young and handsome dropped-out actor who first left me, then relented and gave me a chance to say no. He finally left in a mildly crazy state of mind. ...I'm still here."

I continued,

"Here? At the Esalen Institute beside the sea, site of youth, freedom of mind, groovy hot sulfur baths filled with real and imagined seduction, wild mountain folk who dropped out of North Beach back in the days of Ginsberg. The sea, the sky, and steep, steep hills. I'm very glad to be alive, the drama of life intrigues me and I want to be a part of it and play my role to the hilt. In short, I know something about me now, and consequently I know something about everything else."

I woke up from my technicolor dream to find I was actually employed by Esalen Institute. I pinched myself. Nope, not a dream. Real.

On my second day at work in the Esalen Kitchen I was carefully chopping more carrots than I had ever seen and banging lettuces stem side down like a karate champion to make the leaves easily fall away. "Never wash a knife, just wipe it off and put it away." I twisted each orange slice and graced each plate with a sprig of slightly wilted parsley. Voilà! Food preparation was instant art: You make it; you present it; it's over and you're onto the next meal. When I got my first paycheck—I'd worked 12 days in a row—I bought my own sleeping bag that actually zipped, cementing my independence.

Some of my under-the-bridge dinner pals were in a yearlong experiential workshop called the Residence Program. They invited me to sit in on their group. After their winter together, I knew they wanted fresh blood. I don't admire head trippers; I want magic and authenticity, "LSD and Revolution and God," as Paul Krasner wrote in the SF *Oracle* newspaper published on Haight Street. Those were my values. Could those align with Esalen's well-manicured lawns and paying guests at the seminars where they just sat around? More to the point, could I align with the residents' group who'd invested eight months of their lives to live at Esalen and sit at the feet of a multitude of thought leaders? They hadn't really dropped out. Yet they'd coughed up thousands of dollars for this program and then found themselves working to save the place. That spelled some sort of commitment, I conceded.

Truth, the residents scared me. I preferred to think my way through problems, relying on myself. To the contrary, they were engaged in a different revolution, focusing on the knowledge that comes through our senses and on accepting rather than fighting change, more interested in taking over the culture instead of dropping out of it. They were learning about groups and how groups of people behave. Was this another way to build a revolution? Or a community? I'd come to Esalen seeking a way out of the breakdown that I'd witnessed in the anti-war movements. Now I was challenged to dig deeper into myself instead of lashing out at a seemingly alien America.

At Esalen, workshop leaders like Claudio Naranjo, Jack Downing, and Will Schutz encouraged acting out, meaning I'd be sharing my dark thoughts with others. In my second class with Claudio, he extolled the wisdom of confession, and then invited us, in groups of two, to do just that. I listened intently to my partner, a dropped-out priest. He expressed his discomfort with his daily thoughts of sex and masturbation practice. Did I...? I blushed, "Of course not." My turn: I had nothing to confess. Well, nothing that I was willing to share as confessional. I couldn't—wouldn't—put my faults on display. But still, the possibilities tantalized me. I brushed off my embroidered jeans, blinked my blue eyes, and picked my way carefully up to the meeting room for the next class.

I could stop right here. I didn't come to Esalen to inspect myself. Yet Esalen was seeping into me, changing me. I could make do with this establishment, especially this Esalen management staffed by a noted local ceramicist, an enamel artist cum poet who said to me, "Esalen could have gone either way, to an arts center or toward psychology." My co-workers included a classical guitarist and a self-styled jeweler. The head of security was designing a new tarot deck, and one chef gave us tarot readings in exchange for a glass of port. My luncheon salad contributions were acceptable to the paying guests. The kitchen management rotated unexpectedly every three months. All those plates out the back door cut into their profit margin. The only real culinary vibe in the kitchen was supplied by Ricardo, the gay Filipino bartender who kept up the music protocol — classic Vivaldi at breakfast — and knew how to find a new local cook when the old one threw all the plates. "I work here," I lifted my chin and shared with the inquiring women in the hot tub.

My first work-shift started the day the new Esalen kitchen opened, remodeled to be bigger, better, clean, and rodent-free. Management had been forced to replace the former wooden lean-to when its sagging floor began to show drafty holes. The new tile floor underfoot gleamed, but its hard surface pained our sandaled feet. The wood countertops felt comfy and organic, though we needed to get out the bleach to keep the stains at bay. We cleaned the dining tables with vinegar water and scrapped away the candlewax that dripped from the wine bottle candle holders, the only source of light. The acid vinegar dissolved the pearls in my outdated wedding ring.

My co-workers in the kitchen knew even less than I did about kitchen work, yet we churned out a hot breakfast with eggs and Canadian bacon, a salad and entrée lunch, and a dinner of salad, meat, a veggie, rice, and — my contribution — dessert. The baker made thick wheaty bread so good it was famous up and down the coast. We waitresses, in our handcrafted long flowing skirts, composed the peach cobbler: canned peaches, yellow cake (mix).

We tried unsuccessfully to create bread pudding. Each morning, at 8:30 am, we smiled as we poured coffee and delivered the plates of scrambled eggs. This table service continued throughout the day. As Esalen grew more crowded, hungry seminarians had to wait their turn, resulting in shouting matches between the very folks who were leading groups on equanimity. It was not unknown to see a waitress hurl a glass of wine at a seminarian who complained too loudly. Self-expression was exalted and we took full advantage.

The staff sat at their own table refusing to mingle with the "uptight" guests. Fritz Perls lorded over a table with Selig Morganrath, designer and head of the maintenance Department, and Ken Price, a down to earth, jack-of-all-trades fellow who had watched over nearby Tassajara Zen Mountain Center a year earlier. He knew everything and enjoyed an argument. Pity the poor fourth person who sat at that table! Of course, we served them first. "Staff have to get to work," we justified. Fritz repaid the favor by frequently circling through the kitchen, freely hugging any of us young waitresses or offer up a quivery kiss. We giggled and turned the other cheek, sharing tales later about his frisky playfulness with staff and women in his groups. No one would have called this harassment.

As providence would have it, my second guest class with the residents brought together my East Coast College experience and today's wrangler world of Esalen residents seeking enlightenment. In 1964, the Princeton Neuropsychiatric Center had experimented with LSD and alcohol addiction recovery. They'd hired several of my Rutgers pals to act as aides, though none of them got to actually take the LSD. Now the mastermind of the clinic, H. A. Abramson, was here at Esalen, to talk about his experience and to show off his other skill, hypnosis. I was invited to join the class and participate in his group trance. I was the newcomer to the group. I didn't really have a lot of trust built up yet. So, when he talked about trance, I thought about how I wasn't going to get hypnotized. I'd stay in this zone of consciousness, thank you. A faintly rotund man in his 50's, he counted down and altered our vision so that we saw out of just one eye. I went along with this, agreeing to forego eyesight in my right eye. Suddenly the world had no depth. My curiosity slowly swung toward alarm.

After he brought us out of the trance, we shared about our experience of openness or paranoia. I kept my mouth shut. I had my rules. My feelings were to be sorted out and monitored before sharing. What would people think? I felt embarrassed for one of my bridge buddies when he cried as he described his fear of being closed in. The group drew closer to him. I looked away. I hadn't learned yet that tears were not shameful here, but honest expression, a release.

Then Dr. Abramson came to each of us quietly and asked, "What do you want? "

"I just want more space." I responded easily. I instantly felt the world broaden. Cool! Yet I needed more. I didn't know yet to mention love.

Sex Will Save Us

Sex was a major player in this youthful community. The three-pronged trident of the birth control pill, women's liberating claim on their orgasm, and Huxley's **Island** linking the senses, spirituality and tantra drove home a new morality. Instead of abstinence, pleasurable sexual relations would pave the way to physical wellbeing and a free psyche. When I arrived in the kitchen for the breakfast shift at 7:30 with dark circles under my eyes and a testy attitude, my co-worker Ellen loudly proclaimed, "She just needs to get laid." This sensibility – sex was the answer to every ill, and without it I'd be uptight and unhealthy – pervaded our staff culture and was the envy of midwestern seminarians. What's more, once a relationship got steamy, I shouldn't say "no." That would screw up our natural impulses. Somehow, I must manage to navigate between no inhibitions and heartfelt relationships.

At the same time, Esalen was a fishbowl. When your best beau walked into the lodge with a new flushed woman behind him, you knew what had come down. Sex. Just as much as we professed an open attitude responding, "Do whatever you want!" when asked by a cute redhead if she could spend the night with my boyfriend because, "we've got a lot in common," jealously frequently raised its ugly head, resulting in slaps, workplace retaliations, and real pain. So, I learned to be caution around my affections, to keep my liaisons out of sight, and to yell and hit. "Did you fuck ....?" Paul had angrily accused me the preceding year. Bam! I pushed back, turned and ran, and kept distance for an hour or two while we got over it.

Now, I was one of the few single women on campus. I learned to duck out of sight and use the shadows to dodge the nearly panting workshop participant and the old timer at the gate who saw me as fresh meat. The shared staff quarters put a further crimp on coupling. When the musician I had enchanted on the dance floor entered our tiny cabin and kissed the wrong girl, she screamed and the jig was up. Just as startled, he backed out the door and caught a ride home to his wife.

I took more workshops, invited in for free. Gestalt? I described it in a letter: "A group…a chair…a psychiatrist. Each person sitting in the chair works for maybe half an hour and then sits down in the outer ring again… Working consists of either acting out dreams by playing all the parts, (always described in the present tense) or else simply going more deeply into where you are right now. One "young chick" in the one group didn't want to work because she didn't trust the men in the group (middle class businessmen in their 50's) so she had to go around the room and tell them all individually just that." I added that this instruction shocked me at the time, but I couldn't fail to notice how she changed in each interaction and softened as the men became real to her. So did the seduction plan that one of the men had tucked into his suitcase. Later I wrote "It's therapy directed totally to here and now. The result is often tears, anger, whatever trip you're on. This clears the scene of a whole lot of shit and frees you to do what you really want to do." If we had a goal, that was it: to find our true path in life, to be *authentic*, whatever that was.

In one gestalt group I worked on my recurring dream of being chased by policemen. The leader had a heyday. "Be the policeman. Who does he remind you of?" I was scared. I was angry. I recognized him. I became indignant and raised my voice. "I've moved to California to get away from your rules!" I shuddered, and as I did so, I became aware of the imagined bindings around my chest and took a huge breath to dislodge them. I literally felt them slip away. I've never had that dream again.

No doubt about it, Esalen was the place to be now. During the summer we witnessed Ringo and George from the Beattles arriving with the Maharishi in a helicopter on the front lawn during one of our kitchen breaks. We set our knives aside and hurried down to witness this surprise event. Fritz gave the Maharishi a few minutes, then pointedly turned and left the lawn.

Another evening Ravi Shankar filled the lodge with his drone sitar that somehow transported me to other worlds. For this concert I preferred to listen outside on the deck, still not comfortable sitting on the floor with those "straights".

These celebrity moments came and went, each its own entourage and disembodied hype. I preferred our local entertainment. Several nights a week we danced wildly after hours, to vinyl records of Janis Joplin, the Chambers Brothers, and, whenever possible, to the live drums, guitar, piano, string base, and flute of the local musicians. My long skirt whirled, my scant crocheted top swung, and I tapped the faster beat with my bare feet. Old stuck places within me freed as I moved into my own dance, keeping my eyes open to avoid a collision. I shyly joined the musicians — outside, where I couldn't be heard--on my end-blowing bamboo flute. I didn't need to sleep – or to wake from this new larger-than-life technicolor movie with a great soundtrack.

Touch Me Heal me

During my dinner shift, I dodged the incoming guests as I rushed to deliver a fresh salad bowl to a distant table. I scurried around a short fortyish blonde woman who stood hugging a much taller greying man, her long loose dress pressed against his body. A few minutes later I dodged her again, this time as she stood in lengthy embrace with a young dark-haired woman. I changed my course and averted my eyes. This kind of deliberate hug behavior made me uncomfortable. This was too public a display of affection. I mean, weren't these feelings meant to be private!

Still, I witnessed an ongoing display of hugs, arms thrown over shoulders, and tender backrubs around me at Esalen. I managed to sidestep Seymour's bear hug and the surprise smooch, but the occasional jab, "Hey, Brita, what are you? Up tight?" began to come home. No doubt about it; I was uptight about touch.

My Scandinavian family displayed affection without a lot of physical contact or, in my view, clinging. As a young adult, I narrowed touch down to sexual invitation or maybe comforting the ill. The hug I gave my beloved former college roomy when we met up in San Francisco was a quick embarrassed embrace with a glance over her shoulder. Touch was a skill I clearly lacked, but I didn't know how or where to learn it. Somehow reading about it didn't seem to confront the issue.

When I heard that Molly Day Schackman was presenting a two-part introductory massage class – one week followed later by a second week – I jumped in. She was the top massage practitioner on the massage staff. I watched her give a massage on the wooden tables at the baths. She moved around the table like a martial artist, slow, leaning far over her client and pausing her hands like a masterful pianist. She knew what she was doing. Originally a Swedish Massage practitioner, she took the sensory awareness work of Charlotte Selver to heart and paid more attention to the overall effect of her work. With my very Swedish name and blue eyes, I was frequently asked "What's Swedish Massage?" I didn't have a clue. I didn't know it was based on a therapeutic model, where the practitioner squeezed muscles and encouraged the blood flow up the legs." Swedish Massage?" said Paul. "Oh, they're the ones who wear white jackets. And white shoes."

Sensory awareness: I knew what that was. I'd seen those groups on the lawn, with Bernie Gunther at the lead. A young man sat on the grass at the head of an elderly woman lying comfortably in front of him. He gently cradled her head in his outstretched hands for a minute, and ever so slowly lifted it an inch or two upward, and then ever so slowly guided it back down. She sighed very deeply and lay still. Minutes later they huddled heads together while she spoke softly with him. He nodded, without words. She rolled over, still in slow motion, and took his place while he claimed her spot on the lawn. It looked terribly intimate to me, and scary. Holding someone's head! Could I do that? What if I dropped it?

My turn came, a week later. "Just let your head sink into my hands," gently toned my partner, Bernie himself. I tried, but nothing changed. Nope, I didn't know how. After multiple tries, I succumbed – that's what it felt like, surrender – and I felt a sense of spaciousness descend over me as my head returned effortlessly to the earth. But wait. Wasn't I supposed to hold onto my head, to keep it together? My spacious moment evaporated. I lifted my head and shared my experience with my partner. He made it clear: awareness was the name of this game. We tried it again and this time I focused attention on my body, the tickling grass, the sound of children in the pool – and here was the biggest shift – consciously let go of the back of my neck all the way up to my hairline. My deep sounded sigh said it all. As my head sank into the lawn for the last time, I remembered Aldous Huxley, in **Island,** and the repeating call, "attention, Attention!" I'd read that book last year and thought it was just about the sex.

I scanned the handwritten notice Molly thumbtacked to the message board, advertising her upcoming class. *"We will focus on becoming centered and quiet, learning to move from our center, and allowing the inner power we have achieved to flow naturally and caringly through our hands to the bodies of others, awakening their senses."* I didn't want to practice massage—touching strangers sounded icky—but this could maybe teach me how to touch, in a familiar classroom setting. While the massage I received from Paul was pleasant, his percussive pummeling on my back put me on edge, like being attacked by grasshoppers. I wanted to learn this stuff, to cut the pummeling and add the longer strokes. So, I signed up. I set my compass to the class and joined nine other staff members on the South side of the baths, united in the moist air, fragrant with sulfur. Trying to appear nonchalant, I took the group in. OK. Two guys on conscientious objector leave from Antioch University, my gal co-worker from the kitchen, another staff member I didn't know, and so on. This looked safe enough. I scanned for the hugging woman. She wasn't in the class.

We stood in a naked semi-circle around Molly, a wrapped towel covering our privates. She was a trim, dark-haired woman in her late 30's, professional in her demeanor, clear in her directions. She wore a light cotton blouse, tucked in, and color coordinated pants. She looked us over and paused. "OK, let's take a breath." I felt my mind quiet as I followed this all-to-simple suggestion. She checked our names off and began her demonstration.

Though later she would start the massage session face up, she opened today's class with her massage model, a class member, face down. She rubbed her hands together and urged us to do the same. I carefully became aware of the space around my hands and sure enough I felt the hum of something I might call energy. Whew! Now she gently rested her hands mid-back. "I'll just follow his breathing," she intoned. She wasn't doing anything, just resting there. This looked scarier than I'd imagined. Doing nothing! This doing nothing part of the demonstration gave me time to take in the sound of the waves, the cry of a sea bird, and the lowering of the sun on the horizon. But still…how could doing nothing be part of a massage?

Molly picked up her clove-scented oil bottle, squeezed several drops into her hand, warmed it by rubbing her hands together, and began to apply it in long rhythmic strokes over her partner's back. She made it look effortless, in tune with the ocean. But how would I know where to go? What if it felt bad? Or hurt? My mind screamed, "Can't this wait until tomorrow?" Somehow the word "class" had not indicated that we were actually going to learn to give and experience a massage. I was jolted out of my thoughts by her next words, "Now pick a partner."

I had to make a choice here, to receive touch from one of my classmates or to apply the oil myself onto someone's naked backside. Molly looked around at our anxious faces. She slowly unpacked our fears, offering us the advice to follow the contours of the body with flowing strokes, and – most importantly – quiet our minds so that we could use our intuition. "There's no pattern," she repeated. "Start anywhere."

So, I said "Yes" to one of the Antioch boys, agreed to give first, and realized that learning by sensing another person was an alltogether new way of building a relationship. I let my hands rest on his mid-back and wait, listen, for his breath pattern to steady so that I knew I was well-received. I sought to develop my own pattern: feel my partner, respond through my hands, note my partner's reaction--yes, he's still breathing, nice and even—and move on. I attempted to mimic the woman in front of me as she applied the oil, but her partner was big and hairy and mine was short and slight, so I had no recourse but to chart my own path. Back, legs, arms, neck all received their dose of oil. My hands began to feel the muscles beneath the skin, and I could see the contours of his calf muscles soften. His body was shifting. "How's that feel?" I asked my partner who responded with a thumbs up. Afterward I checked: did it hurt? My sense of the body fell into two categories: pleasure-usually sexual—and pain. This might be something else. Awareness?

"No pain," he assured me. "I did feel some old tension in my legs, but it seemed to dissolve under your touch." I didn't have words to respond. I smiled inwardly, shy about this news. I had played a part in his feeling better.

Now came my turn to lie on the table. While I reasoned that a massage and touching bare skin might deliver a sexual invitation, I vowed to draw clear boundaries with this youth, barely a man. I smiled at him and mentioned my stiff neck. This would be good, I told myself. I felt less comfortable about being touched by a woman. I didn't have a cuddly relationship with my mother. More to the point, despite my professed open mind I didn't want to be portrayed as a dyke. A lesbian. No, I'd stick to massaging men.

His first-time massage session worked its magic on me once I got over lifting my head to see what he was doing. This relaxation business almost made sense. I stayed extra aware as he massaged my lower back, up my legs. But these strokes were circular in nature, following the limb up and then returning to the starting point on my ankle without hinting of closeness to my private parts. I finally gave in and stopped monitoring his every move. I drifted on the waves, felt the breeze touch my body, heard the soft murmur of my classmates. "We're done," he whispered in my ear, then backed away while I regrouped, grabbed my towel, and sat up, beyond words. I couldn't even give him feedback.

The next class I had no other choice but to work with a woman. Still, none of my classmates looked at me funny, or implied I was gay. Checking with her was out of the question. In fact, I barely looked at her. I plunged ahead. After that opening pause and the initial long strokes, I grew to appreciate the different form and muscles of the feminine body. "Just follow the contours." I learned bodies came in all shapes, textures, and sizes. And moods, apparently.

The psychology-focused group leaders at Esalen were all students in Ida Rolf's pioneering deep bodywork training — Jack Downing, Will Schultz, Beverly Silverman. Why? I wondered. Psychology dealt with the mysterious all-important mind. Who paid attention to the body? Yet these seminal leaders gave up months of their lives to study bodywork and its effect on body and psyche. The body must be more central than I realized. Could its release affect our mental well-being? This seemed preposterous, yet these shrinks claimed they were witnessing it right before their eyes. They were writing books about it, too. "Every thought in the mind is reflected in the body," stated best-selling author of JOY, psychologist Will Schutz.

A copy of Atlantic Monthly landed in the staff mailbox. In it, an article titled "How America Lost Its Mind" echoed my surprise regarding the importance of the body. The author, Kurt Anderson, summed it up and quoted one of the founders, "Esalen was a pilgrimage center for...thousands of youth interested in... breakthrough consciousness, the sexual revolution, encounter, being sensitive, finding your body, yoga — all of these things were at first filtered into the culture through Esalen...making a world impact."

I survived both massage classes. I sought a textbook recipe for massage and Molly didn't want to give me one. "Use your intuition," she briskly admonished me. How was I supposed to learn how to massage if I was using my own intuition! Thinking and memorization played second fiddle in her world. Very slowly I begin to follow "hunches" within the massage session. My partner asked how I knew that was the spot. I just smiled.

Giving a Massage

I hesitated to ask my friends if they'd be willing to lie on my massage table because I was such a novice. Yet I needed practice, so I took a chance. My first inquiry yielded, "Hey, yeah!" and he almost slipped off his shirt on the spot. The southside of the bathhouse with its plank tables was open for our use. The sulfur springs gurgled merrily, and the ocean waves hit the shoreline a hundred feet below the outer fence. The corrosive element of the sulfur steam left dark stains on the cement block tubs and the water trough. The hot tubs heated the air up enough to make for an enjoyable atmosphere. I stepped over a greenish slick — mold? — on the cracked cement floor and set up my table with a sheet, towel, and oil, all purloined from the bathhouse massage supply closet. The sun was still high over the western horizon, painting the southern cliffs, baths and my table in golden light.

"Yes, this afternoon?" responded Don, when asked if he wanted a massage. A former Marine with a short stocky body, he was new to bodywork; relaxing would be a novel experience for him. Only when he lay face down and I got a good look at his back did I realize what I had failed to notice: he had muscles. Lots of them. OK. My focus deepened. After those opening long strokes. I climbed up onto the tabletop, standing over him, to gain leverage. I could bend forward and drop all my weight onto my hands and then slowly trace his back on either side of his spine. "Ohhhh," he moaned with apparent pleasure. I could move his tissue, offer him relief from a day of loading firewood. Climbing down from the table, I gingerly dropped into his muscles with my hands, my weight. I could see shift in his contours; I could relieve his tired back. A Vietnam vet, his normally bull-like structure seemed to be more flexible now. Afterward I felt calm, not tired. He lay on the table a long time, digesting this session maybe. Was he ok? When

Giving a Massage

he finally rolled over, stretched out a leg, and finally sat upright, he breathed, "What *was* that?" And smiled. Something about giving a massage quieted me down, too, and put me into a space like a color-enhanced dream, beyond time. Childlike, we friends joined hands as we slowly walked up the hill, the sky rosy with sunset steaks coloring the waves a new shade.

I practiced my massage skills on the psychiatrist Jack Downing between his classes with Ida Rolf. For this session I set up in the sparse cinderblock massage room lit with 14 candles to provide heat and a flickering light reminiscent of long-ago caves. The broad front windows opened to the sea, and the massage table height fit me. Dressed in my blue Danskin leotard, I warmed my hands together and arranged the clove-scented oil on the windowsill. Honestly, I was scared. I admired Jack, an MD by training, and I knew about Rolfing, a very deep bodywork method that required extensive knowledge of muscles and bones. I didn't study any of that stuff. Yet when I called him out of the hot tub and up the few steps into the room, he readily shared his personal experiences with me, asking me what I felt and what I noticed about his body. During the massage I became witness to his process of holding and releasing. "That's something else I can let go of," he intoned with a sigh as his leg visibly relaxed. He didn't tell me what it was. As Ida said, the process took care of itself; no need to add words or story. I rested my hands on his feet, giving us both a moment of stillness.

When I gazed over the vast curve of ocean, following Molly's instructions to take in the energy of place, I felt the tingle of spirit light up my body, an undeniable experience of unity far beyond new age jargon. After my hands lifted, Jack rested a minute, then swung his legs smoothly off the table. The peaceful set of his jaw and softness around his eyes said far more than his humble "Thank you."

I started to receive as many sessions as I could to better understand what this thing called bodywork or massage was all about. The following year when I received my first deep Rolfing session, my ribs fought back when stern hands suggested they could loosen their immobile street-smart protectiveness. Ouch! The following moment I took the deepest breath I can ever remember, and I giggled. I didn't need that armor anymore. A day later, the freedom was still with me and my shirt barely buttoned around my ribs. I was changing, no doubt about it.

What about the allegations about touchy-feely, the notion that massage was just selfish pleasure? Was I selling out to spa mentality? I came to the Haight and then to Esalen seeking a new way to bring peace to communities and the world, expelling the old political habit of churning out angry words that didn't change anything. I respected this unspoken contract between peoples who saw the potential for a deeper response, more than just a legislative fix. What if we could all just touch each other, recognize each other's vulnerability, heal each other? Something about touch reminded me I was human, embodied, like my close friend and also that pro-war demonstrator down the street. This acceptance of the human body in its nakedness, this notion that touch can heal, stood in strong relief against my parents' and my college profs' world, in mid-sixties' culture. Even my radically inclined ex couldn't see any point to massage, touch without an erogenous goal.

This became my preferred conversation, communicating through touch, recognizing what my friend's body was saying, rather than just hearing their words. I slowly became comfortable with touch, with giving and receiving massage. I described my experience in a letter to my friend Miki, "It's like a concentrated meditation and mellows me out."

Affirmation from the Astral Plane

I booked a private psychic reading session with Anne Armstrong, an intuitive group leader at the Institute. Ann was more than a psychic; she worked informally for NASA through her scientist husband. When the rocket fuel system fizzled, she reportedly ran it through her body and diagnosed the problem. If the government could do it, I could certainly give her powers a try on my own situation. My guy was gone; something was off. What was my life calling?

A pert small woman with neat gray hair, her eyes looked weary today. We sat on the floor, facing each other. Ann wasted no time. Without really responding to my opening question, she began to share details about my current path in life. I was surprised to travel with her as she journeyed into the psychic world. It was almost as if we elevated together to a vantage point somewhere above the room in which we were sitting. She momentarily stopped talking and looked at me. "I feel very relaxed in your presence." She paused, almost as if to take in this pleasurable sensation, and her face looked brighter. "Have you ever considered joining the massage crew?" I breathed in her question, felt it enter my body and find a home. I hadn't even mentioned this possibility.

I invited her intuition to guide me, move me toward this decision, reach far beyond my reasoning mind, as if my brain softly expanded. My doubts lost traction; I could do this. Not only did practicing massage fit my mission of influencing world peace but I could set my own hours. My social worker background agreed. Most of all, my close friends had already moved on from waitressing to giving massages down in the hot springs. I, instead, had moved onto becoming a secretary, administrative assistant to

Affirmation from the Astral plane

the soft-spoken director, Ben Weaver. This inside job track excited and exhausted me. The mental negotiating with the Esalen community and the hungry American culture left no time for me. The pay was good. Yet when my boss quit, so did I.

Over the next year I signed onto every kind of bodywork session available at Esalen. I received Rolfing, polarity, Esalen massage, shiatsu. Each session opened me to an unexplored aspect of myself. I recognized how I limped like my polio survivor father even though I had no physical impairment. Rolfing balanced my hips. Sometimes tears I could not explain brimmed out my eyes. Letting go of my head to relax into my partner's hands still felt dangerous; yet me neck felt flexible and swan-like when I succumbed. I studied massage with everyone – Jill Harris, Gabrielle Roth, Ida Rolf's students, the psychics – and finally I felt comfortable enough to try out for the crew. "I'm not sure I ever really had a massage before," breathed my evaluator as he struggled to sit up and give his report. Two test massages later I was hired.

I covered my typewriter and bought a new leotard. I wrote, "Miki, I'm good enough now that I can get all but the most uptight out of their preoccupied head and into a pleasant NOW state in an hour and a half of good bodywork. My understanding of both physiognomy (sic) and energy patterns (like the Indian system of Chakras) is getting a lot better."

Fast forward one year. My friend and head of the massage staff, Peggy Horan, talked me into co-leading a workshop titled "Body Music." After my resisting, "I'm not ready," she prevailed. When the sixteen students arrived – all types of men and women, a police officer on a break – I rode their infectious enthusiasm for something as out-of-the-box as learning to massage each other in a non-sexual, agenda-free way. I pulled it off famously and sailed into a new career, joining a few brave souls who made their way to Esalen to break the touch barrier. As for my first goal – to learn to hug – I'd like to say "just spread your arms out wide and I'm in." Closer to the truth, most every hug starts for me with a moment of reckoning, a quiet "you can do this," and then the delight of truly meeting another human, belly to belly.

How Do You End a Chapter

I have walked that long road to freedom...I have taken a moment here to rest, to steal a view of the glorious vista that surrounds me, to look back on the distance I have come. But I can only rest for a moment, for with freedom come responsibilities, and I dare not linger, for my long walk is not ended. Nelson Mandela, **Long Walk to Freedom**, 1994.

There's a quiet in my cottage. Even the gnarled overhanging oak ceases to rattle its leaves. The crows have moved from my deck to the tops of the nearby redwood tree. No click of the keypad. No foot falls. Just the sound of breathing. My deep uneven sigh. I've reached a pause in my story, my personal story.

How do you end a chapter? With a break-up? A birth? A change of career? A landslide closes Route One and traffic stops? With death? I could check all those boxes. Paul died of a heart attack at age fifty-four, sheltering in a Pacific Grove backyard. In this unpainted shack swept clean, his single mattress was laid out on the rough wood floor. One of those scratchy wool Mexican rugs, striped in gray, black and spice red lies folded neatly upon it. But he's missing. The empty wine jug sits in the corner, capped with a chipped enamel metal cup. A pen lies open on the floor. The wood plank walls are bare except for a drawing by the little boy next door. Paul's own art is posted in a stationary store in Carmel Crossroads, a flower shop in Monterey, a restaurant in Pacific Grove. But he's dead now. Alcohol, poverty, lack of medical attention. His mental baggage from Hollywood failures proved too much for his heart. Or maybe he spent all those years in search for love to replace the love I extended. I didn't want to know. The town threw a memorial in honor of this notable character at a wharf restaurant. I didn't go. Unfinished.

Or should I end with the future chapter, the surprise global success of Esalen® Massage? Right now, three practitioners are bending over their tables at the Esalen mineral baths, waves crashing on the boulders below. Their slow pace and attentive strokes speak directly to their partner's nervous system. With a shudder or deep sigh, the prone bodies recalibrate, and I can see from afar the sudden drop of the shoulders, the toes unfurling, the softer jawline. The body! This is where my year on the mountain comes home, the connection with this Big Sur land, earth meeting heaven, right through each one of us. Our body.

Or should I end more personally, with today's family and yesterday's divorce? "Were you a hippie?" my granddaughter interrupts, as she springs through the door.

"Yes," I respond proudly, sitting taller. I hand her a gift I unearthed at the local second-hand store: a paisley swirly skirt to fit her narrow teen frame. She spun around, just as my daughter Ivy spun so often in her youth at Esalen. Yes, I wore my hair long and tied beads around my neck; I marched with Dr. King, confronted war politicians, made regular pilgrimages to City Lights Bookstore, lived off the grid in a tent, enlivened my spirituality with psychedelics, danced until the musicians went home. I took up the challenge of honest relationship, gave up the nice-girl smile, admitted I was scared. I smiled at her. "Yes." I repeated out loud. She danced away, swishing her new skirt. The door slammed.

Cash reality shook hands with me in Motherhood. I persisted in my mission to practice this massage that insisted the human body had its own wisdom to heal. My touch invited presence and I stepped back to let change happen. We became teachers to practitioners. We gathered up sheets, towels and oil in our arms and headed downhill to the bathhouse tables with a group of sixteen trailing behind us. We taught in the sunlight and in the fog. We started something and it grew to something else. Women stood tall and proud in their bodies; men learned to let their chests soften with emotion. Love.

Steeped

The mountains dropping into the sea, the earthy smell of redwood and most of all the floaty mineral-stinking water of the hot springs made it all possible.

There will be other chapters. I am my own worst student when it comes to trusting my intuition, loving my body and its passions, welcoming this messy life. I know this beyond a doubt: It is my experience lived out, acted on, shared and molded by you that makes a difference more meaningful than this line of words.

Sunbeams slant through in my open window and the birdsong takes a pause. The ruddy-colored singer who holds forth from my light wire is now nestled somewhere up in the swaying limbs. Was she, too, comforted by the sound of rustling leaves, the scent of the bay tree? The voices have gone quiet, too. No students complaining of spiders in the sheets, no lover wondering why I'm still at work — in fact, no lover — and a coterie of youthful teachers ready to change the world through touch. We dreamed big.

I turn up the volume on my nearby radio. Today we have nation more divided than when I dropped out sixty years ago. We experienced a pandemic that killed one million Americans and sent others into a frenzy of noisy jab avoidance. Teens and old folks are depressed, and my friend Kelly has cancer.

Yet the native lupine blooms at the beach's edge in an unimagined cream and lavender and the wild roses burst forth in brief multi-petaled splendor. The breeze buffs my cheeks. Touch. I remember the touch of Paul's eyes, always dancing, leading me here even though we didn't know it. Touch. That's where I fit, in wild harmony with the animal, plant, mineral and human systems that weave together this planet. We can't fix it all, but we can engage, caress and breathe. "Inhale the Prana!" exclaimed Big Sur Bard Patrick Cassidy, as he stood above Hot Springs Canyon, the rich oxygenated air visibly blue above the treetops if I softened my eyes.

I can rest a moment here, let my shoulders relax and my feet still. My hands have typed miles and touched people of every color and temperament. They now lie folded in my lap. My shoes stand outside the door. Ready.

About the Author

Brita Ostrom is a highly respected leader in massage therapy, somatic education, and psychotherapy, best known for her long-standing involvement with the Esalen Institute in Big Sur, California.

Brita has been teaching at the Esalen Institute since the late 1960s, where she has led massage and bodywork workshops for decades. She helped establish the Esalen Massage School and played a major role in shaping the institute's unique approach to bodywork. In addition to her work in massage, she is a licensed psychotherapist and is well-versed in Gestalt awareness practices and somatic education.

Brita's path to Esalen began in the 1960s, inspired by the counterculture movement and the writings of influential thinkers. She became part of the Esalen community during its early years, immersing herself in its experimental and holistic environment. Her experiences there included learning from pioneers in psychology and bodywork, and participating in the institute's creative and communal lifestyle.

Brita Ostrom continues to teach and mentor at Esalen, offering workshops and trainings in massage and somatic practices. She is based in the Big Sur and Marin area of California and remains active in the wellness and personal growth community.

About Coalesce Press

"Coalesce" reflects the mission of Morro Bay's beloved bookstore: *to grow together and unite*. Coalesce Press was established to extend the voices and stories that bring communities closer.

In Memory of Linna Thomas

Linna Thomas embodied the very essence of what made Coalesce Press a beacon for literary voices on the Central Coast, bringing to her publishing endeavors the same gracious spirit, unwavering support, and keen literary instincts that defined her 52 years as the heart of Coalesce Bookstore and Garden Chapel in Morro Bay.

Coalesce Press reflects Linna's deeper understanding that books are not mere commodities but vessels for the "spiritual magic that only occurs when one reads," and she dedicated herself to nurturing that magic by providing authors with not just a publisher, but a friend and advocate who believed in the transformative power of words. *Steeped* would have strongly resonated with Linna.

Learn more at CoalescePress.com

www.ingramcontent.com/pod-product-compliance
Lightning Source LLC
Chambersburg PA
CBHW032037290426
44110CB00012B/835